Walking Up And Down On It: Collected Philosophical Works

Emericus Durden

Radical Academic Press
(an imprint of Party Crasher Press)

"Walking Up And Down On It: Collected Philosophical Works," By Emericus Durden

ISBN-13: 978-0692502167 (Radical Academic Press)
ISBN-10: 0692502165

Radical Academic Press is an imprint of Party Crasher Press. Please direct any enquiries to:
partycrasherpress@gmail.com

Dedicated to every single person who strives to become more than a mere human being

Table of Contents

I.
Aiming Higher Than Mere Civilization: How Skeptical Nihilism Will Remind Humanity Of Its Long Forgotten Purpose

Contents

Part I: Background and Theory

1. *Why do people resist being awakened so?*

The goal of this book is to wake people up – to awaken them from the sleep of their most cherished beliefs and allow them to become the sole authorities over their own lives.

Before I explain why I think people are asleep in the first place and whether I think they *should* be awakened, I must explain what's involved in "waking" someone from the "dream of their beliefs" and why they so strongly resist it.

Much like waking someone from a real sleep requires that you disturb them, with loud noises, for example, or a physical jolt, waking someone from the dream of their beliefs also requires a disturbance, though here the disturbance is an emotional and intellectual one, not so much a physical interaction. Still, a disturbance of some kind is needed.

The need for a disturbance makes waking someone difficult because *no one likes to be disturbed and therefore everyone resists being awakened*. That resistance makes waking someone a rather unpleasant process for both the person doing the waking and the person being awakened. The former feels frustrated by the "inertia" of the latter, while the latter wants only to avoid going through an experience they suspect will be disorienting, painful, and disruptive to their daily lives.

The person being awakened also resents the fact that another person *apparently* much like themselves is forcing (or only encouraging) them to do something *apparently* against their will. In this day and age of so-called democratic ideals, it's offensive to most people that one human being would *apparently* (and, yes, arbitrarily) impose their will on another, even (or perhaps especially) in the name of waking them from their beliefs.

In the last paragraph, I italicize the word "apparently" to emphasize that things may not at all be what they seem. That is to say, the person being awakened (i.e., the reader) resists the waking process because, in fact, they have deceived themselves into believing they are already awake and "right" about their own lives and therefore in no need of any kind of disturbance.

To sum up the last few paragraphs: *people resist being awakened for two reasons: they want to avoid pain, and they believe they (and only they) are right about themselves.* When I mix in society anywhere on the planet, hardly a minute goes by before one or both of those points of resistance crop up in conversation. Indeed, human beings would seem to base their identities mainly on those two points of resistance.

If you get nothing more out of this book than what I stated in the previous paragraph, you have already benefited yourself far more than you can imagine (unfortunately). But if you meet me halfway and proceed, completing the entire book, practicing the exercises described herein, you will do far more than merely benefit yourself: you will transform your "self" into something beyond and yet inclusive of humanity as we know it, into some "thing" higher than this world, for which we have no name, of which we may not speak directly, and yet which "controls," in a real sense, everything that happens in human life.

In brief, by transforming the reader into "something else beyond humanity," the exercises in this book give the reader complete control over their human lives, making it no longer necessary they rely on the authority of people or things beyond their own mind and body.

For the purposes of this book, then, *the phrase "being awakened from the dream of one's beliefs" is synonymous with the phrase "becoming something else beyond humanity."*

The latter phrase may sound grandiose, crazy, perhaps incomprehensible, perhaps a bit awkward. But I will let it stand for now, as it communicates the flavor or "taste" of existence after one awakens. That taste is a mix of the high and the low, the human and divine, the sane and insane, the rational and incomprehensible. You will recognize that taste instinctively, because you have tasted it many times before (though you've long forgotten "when"). And once you do taste it, you will no longer need me or this book at your side. You will then be on your own, as it were, yet in complete control. However, until then, a guide along the way might be a tremendous benefit and serve to accelerate your growth. That's where this book enters the picture.

So if, as I say, "becoming something else beyond humanity" means complete control over one's daily life, why would anyone resist it? Stated in that way, the accomplishment sounds quite attractive. Well, *people resist the idea of awakening because it contradicts everything they have learned and taken to be true about life – indeed, it contradicts basic common sense.* And by contradicting what they understand to be true, awakening directly threatens people's egos, their identities, the core of what they "know" about themselves and the society they live in.

Awakening thus seems to be a very frightening event, on par with physical death, and indeed it is. To put it most provocatively (but nonetheless accurately), *"waking from the dream of our beliefs" destroys all human knowledge and truth.*

The first implication of awakening is that ***there exists a "higher thing" entirely independent of human beings and other biological organisms***, some "thing" not perceptible or measurable, not material in the sense rocks and flesh are material, and thus beyond the pale of scientific research, inaccessible to its instruments and devices. Consequently, if we want to learn about and experience that "thing," or attempt to confirm or deny its existence, we cannot rely on the fruits of scientific progress. We must reject scientific practice, as it were, and approach the "thing" along a different route of inquiry.

A second implication of awakening is that ***it's possible to transform yourself into that "higher thing,"*** not merely hypothesize or have faith in its existence. Clearly, that implication runs afoul of faith-based religions, which find it sacrilegious to propose that a human being can become or "merge with" a "higher thing" or God, taking on its characteristics and functions.

Finally, most practically and most radically, a third implication of awakening is that, ***having transformed yourself into that "higher thing," you can create whatever world or reality you exist in***, based on your inner visions, imagination, and the focused intentions underlying beliefs you *choose*. As a result, you *control* all aspects of your existence, no longer requiring the direct support of material things like social relationships and money. Obviously that assertion contradicts common sense views of daily life because it implies that *you may control which world you choose to create*.

Given the three implications above in bold, it should be no surprise that "waking from the dream of our beliefs" meets so much resistance. Anyone who even briefly considers the concept – under their current set of beliefs, of course – can only walk away from it shaking their heads, thinking it's the most ridiculous, absurd, and crazy thing anyone has seriously proposed.

History itself would seem to argue against the possibility of awakening. Indeed, as we'll see shortly, a fourth implication of the idea is that ***centuries of so-called "progress" have, in fact, been quite the opposite, a steady retrogression and reduction in our creative abilities***. Rather than a belief we are the active creators of the world we exist in, we have, in the name of progress, chosen a belief (without realizing it) that we are reactive participants in a universe governed by impersonal, random physical forces. Clearly, the latter is a highly "limiting" kind of belief compared to the former.

In fact, it's even worse than that. As a civilization, we have collectively forgotten that a belief like "we are biological organisms at the mercy of impersonal, random physical forces" is, in fact, shorthand for a whole set of "limiting" beliefs we take for granted as obvious truths. Yet we could just as well *choose* to abandon those beliefs, replacing them with a different set of beliefs that support our being creators of the universe rather than reactors to it. In so doing, we would choose beliefs that allow us to see the universe as a place where we are the centers of control, not passive or reactive participants. Importantly, we would make that choice irrespective of the support of scientific evidence.

Clearly, common sense would counter the position I propose above, stating that "the objective truth is not at our discretion to change as we see fit. Truth is not disposable. Simply wanting or intending to be the creator of the universe doesn't make you anything more than a deluded fool." A trained scientist would elaborate on that counterpoint, asserting that a belief like "we are only biological organisms eternally at the mercy of impersonal, random physical forces" is not disposable because it is supported by hard data and evidence gathered and analyzed by brilliant scientists over hundreds of years.

However, both of those responses are themselves reflections of limiting beliefs we may choose to abandon – the first, a belief that the intentions of human beings cannot directly influence the physical universe, and the second, a belief that empirical evidence limits what is possible in daily reality. In fact, once we awaken from the dream of our beliefs, we have the choice of discarding those two beliefs much as we might also discard beliefs in entities like God, angels, and spirits.

It should be clear by now that when I speak of "waking from the dream of our beliefs," I mean waking from the dream of *all* our beliefs, even those beliefs we consider "obvious" or "established" truths about the universe. The great difficulty here is that we may fail to awaken from some deep-seated beliefs if we don't recognize them as beliefs but continue to take them as truths beyond the pale of rational doubt. Therefore, a good part of this book's project consists of inspecting the entire scope of our understanding of life and the universe, our entire intellectual heritage including common sense, and throwing it all into doubt.

The reader should now see why the project I'm proposing generates such strong resistance. In one fell swoop, our entire knowledge base will be overturned, scrapped as it were, reduced to a field of persuasion and disposable beliefs, leaving us without a foundation of truth, feeling confused, disturbed, disoriented. Everything we learned from our parents, teachers and so-called "experts" is reduced to a shifting terrain of unfounded beliefs any one of which we may stand on for awhile and arbitrarily deem "true" before leaping off, at our whim, and standing on another so-called "true" belief.

The above view of a universe of "many relatively true beliefs and opinions," by itself, is not new, and would generally be categorized as a form of nihilism. The 19th Century German philosopher Friedrich Nietzsche, for example, espouses the idea in writings throughout his career. Indeed, two centuries before him, French philosopher Rene Descartes proposed the idea of throwing everything into doubt to find where certainty exists, if it exists at all. What's new here is that I put this sort of nihilism to work, as it were, making a useful tool out of it rather than letting it paralyze us.

Nihilism in all its forms is very useful if you know what to do with it and how to act on it. I cannot emphasize this point enough, as it has been lost on Western philosophy from Descartes through Hume to Nietzsche, Wittgenstein, and the postmodern philosophers. All of those brilliant thinkers had the power and persistence of mind to reach the kind of skeptical nihilism I describe above and yet, having reached it, they didn't know what to *do* with that nihilism.

(To be fair to the rest of the world, I should mention that while Western civilization has apparently never understood the real value of nihilism, some other civilizations have made better use if it. See, for example, the writings of Nagarjuna and other Mahayana and Vajrayana Buddhists. Indeed, this book's methods share multiple tangents with Buddhism, though I address those commonalities in other books, not here.)

Indeed, if you simply allow nihilism to paralyze you intellectually, you are not making good use of it. Nor are you appreciating the value of nihilism if you use it as a political rationale to kill people and destroy property. But if you use nihilism as a point of departure from your own humanity, it can help take you far beyond where you ever imagined you might venture – indeed, it can help transform you into something "higher" than humanity itself. *That is what we will do with nihilism here: we will use it as a tool to transform ourselves.*

So given what I've stated above, I ask the reader, "How capable are you *right now* of waking from the dream of *all* your beliefs?"

Each of you who has read this far should pause and think about your answer to that question, because once you start going through this process – and it may last several years – the things, people, and ideas you enjoy and respect, that is, the things, people, and ideas you now *believe* are good, right, and true, will all start losing their sway over you, and in time you will find yourself "in the wilderness" (not necessarily literally, of course). For all that, I assure you this process has a beginning and an end. However, to make it through to the end transformed, you need three basic qualities: *intelligence, courage, and commitment*. High intelligence, by itself, is not sufficient to reach the end. In the course of the transformation process, your mind will break – trust me on that – and you will need the courage and commitment to put yourself back together again. Without those two other qualities, you may be left with a "broken mind."

The last paragraph touches on another key issue here – *trust*. It lurks behind everything I write in this book – not just any trust, but even more difficult (more troubling to the reader): trust in the words of a total stranger. To get anything useful out of this book, *you must be able to trust the words of a total stranger (i.e., the author) despite the fact you may find it irrational and foolish to do so*. By trusting me, you are actively working against the two points of resistance I mentioned earlier: you are doing something that may result in real pain, and you are doing something that acknowledges (even if only implicitly) you may be "wrong" about yourself, who you are, and what you stand for.

The trust issue is front and center in most guided quests and transformational journeys though it's rarely stated as such. Can you trust a guru? Can you trust a Zen master? Can you trust a therapist? When you first walk into their offices, those people are total strangers just as much as I am here. So why should you trust anything they advise when you don't know them at all? What are your *grounds* for trusting them? Where is the *proof* they deserve your trust?

I suspect if gurus, therapists, and self-help coaches assailed their potential clients with those difficult questions, they might scare most of them away. Indeed, focusing on those questions right at the start might serve only to prevent any relationship from forming at all. Yet, the very real uncertainty underlying those questions will find its way into the teaching relationship anyway, eventually triggering "trust issues" that may put the transformation into serious jeopardy.

Trust issues arise because most people have not skeptically investigated the nature of trust itself. When they do investigate it, they find, much to their dismay, that trust between *any and all* human beings is ultimately founded on an empty illusion, a sort of "persuasive social fabrication," if you will. But if that's the case, we ask ourselves, are not all our social interactions founded on an empty illusion and therefore – *could it be?* – not to be taken seriously or abided by?

By now, the astute reader can see where I'm going with this line of reasoning. I'm extending my skeptical nihilism from the realm of scientific and philosophical knowledge to the realm of social relationships. And by pointing out that trust is illusory, I'm implying that trust in a total stranger like myself cannot be any more risky than trust in your spouse or your parents, because every one of those relationships is founded on the same illusion and equally risky. As such, your ultimate choice to trust me rather than them must be founded on nothing more than an unanalyzable hunch. So be it. Going forward the reader and I shall not pretend otherwise.

Let's face it, what I'm doing here is, at bottom, arbitrary: I'm offering the reader help – take it or leave it. Nothing is up for debate (more on that below). So while you might read this book because you're curious to learn what supposedly crazy, outlandish things I have to say, I'd rather you read it because you're interested in changing your life right now. My goal is to influence the reader's behavior in a positive way, not merely to impart facts like a school lecturer. Helping people rise above themselves is the only meaningful thing left for me to do – I've done everything else. However, I can help them only if they *trust* my advice and perform the exercises below. *By doing exactly what I advise in the interim, the reader will paradoxically free himself and herself from the influence of all external authorities (including me) forever.*

Now, before we launch into the actual methods and practices of waking from the dream of our beliefs, I want to address the two questions I mention above in the second paragraph: why I believe people are asleep in the first place and why I believe people should be awakened.

2. *Why do I believe people are asleep in the first place?*

What led me to the belief "people are asleep" is quite distinct from the reason I hold that belief now. I hold the belief now because I "experience" it every moment of my waking life. In other words, *I hold the belief that most people are asleep (and I am awake) based solely on an act of recognition*. I do *not* hold that belief based on a line of reasoning, a logical argument, or scientific data – that's a very important point.

Be that as it may, I was originally led to that belief by a series of events around the age of thirty that had nothing to do with the belief itself. That's because *I could not have had any idea I was asleep until after I had awakened*. That series of events was a culmination of a general trend in my life at the time of increasing skepticism toward knowledge and increasing disgust for daily life.

Over a period of more than a decade, between the ages of 18 and 30, as I asked more and more questions on increasingly "difficult" topics, I discovered fewer and fewer answers to my questions. I systematically inspected and, to a certain degree, mastered all areas of intellectual endeavor – the physical sciences, the social sciences, philosophy, religion, the arts, the humanities, foreign languages – ultimately finding them wanting, unable to address fundamental questions about my own identity and the purpose of the reality I "found" myself in. At the end of that process I was left stranded, with nothing and nowhere to go, intellectually and emotionally paralyzed.

I had, in other words, used the skeptical and nihilistic powers of my mind to undermine itself. Looking back on it now, I think a somewhat more poetic description would be that I had broken out of the prison of my own mind, and in so doing, I also broke out of the prisons of common sense and social norms. And immediately after having escaped from those prisons, I experienced an incredible series of events I am encapsulating in this book as the process of waking from the dream of one's beliefs.

A quick note here: throughout this book I will use metaphors to describe the awakening process. In describing the process as "waking from the dream of our beliefs" I am already resorting to a metaphor. In the previous paragraph I described it as "breaking out of prison," which is also an apt metaphor. Going forward, I will try to stick with the "awakening" metaphor and not mix it with other imagery, lest I confuse the reader. But please understand that the nature of the process lends itself to a variety of metaphorical descriptions some of which I will periodically resort to for making specific points.

Now, because this book is meant to be a guide, not an autobiography, I will not elaborate on the personal nature of the events surrounding my own awakening (though I may in a subsequent publication). The important point here is that never during my twenties did I suspect I was, in some sense, asleep under the influence of my beliefs. Looking back on it now, I realize I could not have suspected as much, given that I had no concept beforehand of what it means to be awake.

In any case, odd as it may sound, that series of events left me with no other option than to embrace the belief that "people or, more broadly, society is asleep." Through a combination of intelligence, courage, and commitment to what I thought was the truth, I had ended up destroying everything human in my path, all possible belief systems and theories except for one, the belief that I am wide awake while everyone around me continues their slumber. Only when I was left with that single belief did I *recognize* that I too had once been asleep but was now fully awake.

Students of philosophy may recognize this situation as having something in common with another metaphor, the Cave Allegory in Plato's Republic. I suppose it is similar in the sense that it implies two types of human beings exist in society – those who are awake (Plato's philosopher who escapes from and then returns to the cave) and those who continue to sleep (Plato's prisoners who remain chained to the cave's walls forever).

Based on my own experience, I would add that the sleepers far outnumber the awakened ones, which is to say it's the former who compose society (and give it its herd qualities) while the latter are marginalized, reduced to outsider status, ignored and ridiculed. Yet it's only the latter who are qualified to awaken the former because it's impossible for two sleepers to awaken one another (by definition).

The difficulties of this paradoxical situation should be obvious by now. If someone is asleep, they cannot realize it, otherwise they would be awake. That means someone else, a total stranger as it were, must inform them of the fact they are asleep. But when a sleeper learns they have been sleeping, they naturally resist the idea, not trusting a stranger to inform them of something so personal as their metaphysical state without themselves already knowing it. As a result, they ignore the awakened one's remarks, keep their sense of identity intact, but continue sleeping. Such is the human condition.

This asymmetric situation I still find shocking. If you're awake, you know it with certainty because you recall the process of your awakening. But if you're asleep, you cannot know it at all because you were born sleeping and remain so and therefore must rely on someone who is awake to inform you of the fact. Indeed, *whether or not you're asleep can never be an object for debate since the language of debate and argumentation is itself a key aspect of the sleep*. Thus, while an awakened one can recognize both sleep and awakening, a sleeper cannot recognize either and likely cannot conceive of the distinction. Again we see the importance of the concept of *recognition* to the awakening process.

Adding still more difficulty to awakening is our tendency to deepen our collective slumber over time *without realizing we are doing so*. This point brings us back to the concept of scientific progress, which is reflected in a general fascination with physical reality, complexity, and a *belief* that the more scientific information and knowledge we have at our disposal, the better our chances of finding what is "true" and "right" for each of us personally and for society as a whole. That is the rationale behind "scientific progress," after all.

Indeed, if there is an unquestioned faith in society today, it is a faith in scientific progress, a faith in generating more and more knowledge using increasingly sophisticated instruments and devices, to improve our understanding of how the universe "works." The fact that no one seriously touts science as a faith similar to a religious faith is our first clue that the "sleep of our beliefs" is an insidious kind of slumber: the longer we believe something and the more people there are who believe it, respect it, and teach it, the less it seems like a belief or a faith, the more it seems to announce itself as an unquestionable and highly reasonable fact.

But as we'll see below, this collective faith in scientific progress is a soporific that lulls us asleep and prevents us from being sufficiently skeptical of our own human abilities. And *it is only by being completely skeptical of the value of human endeavor that we have a chance to transform ourselves into something higher than humanity.*

As an example of the limits of scientific skepticism, a well trained, highly intelligent physicist will be very skeptical *within* the discipline of physics, carefully inspecting and comparing data to generate and test new hypotheses that are logically consistent with accepted hypotheses. However, he will rarely if ever be skeptical enough to step *outside* physics and question the value of the discipline *as a whole*. (This point equally applies to other scientists, chemists, biologists, geologists, etc.) In other words, the physicist does not realize his skepticism stops short of the limits of the discipline he works in and that he could, had he the necessary courage and commitment, persistently question the value not only of physics but of chemistry, biology, and ultimately of all scientific endeavor. He doesn't do that, however, because *his skepticism stops short at the unfounded belief that physics (and scientific evidence generally) is the ultimate arbiter of what is true and false about reality and the universe.*

Please note above where I underline the words "unfounded belief," as this is where science and scientific progress become faiths, exactly where our skeptical attitude "stops." Right there is where complacency sets in, where we have, in effect, fallen asleep. What makes this situation so difficult is that the scientist was never told in so many words that he must take a vow of faith (i.e., arbitrarily adopt the unfounded belief) that scientific progress is the route to the truth. While it's true he cannot remember such a vow because it did not happen, the net of effect of his training, from elementary school classes to earning a doctorate, is *as if* he took that vow. That's because he was never taught to be sufficiently skeptical of the scientific enterprise *as whole* but only to be highly skeptical within it, much like a priest, for example, might be trained to ask questions within a religion but never to question the religion as a whole.

Yet, while it's been intellectually fashionable over the past century or more to stand outside religion, skeptically questioning its value as a whole and embracing atheism, it's hardly fashionable to do the same with science. Indeed, the general scientific attitude has so infiltrated even common sense that few people are motivated to be skeptical about the value of science as a whole. I have thus found, in discussions with scientists and nonscientists alike, a tremendous resistance to expanding one's skepticism to include all of science, past, present, and future.

Nonetheless, anyone with a functioning mind has the real option of throwing all scientific practice into doubt and in so doing to "see" daily reality from a very different perspective. We will do that ourselves in the exercises below. And as we awaken, our brave and committed skeptical nihilism will destroy scientific knowledge and complexity rather than add to it, eventually leaving "us" outside of scientific progress, outside of history, outside of humanity itself. What we "are" there and what we can "do" there we will "see" as we develop along the new route proposed in this book.

Meanwhile, we can expect scientists as a group to resist our project, for at least two main reasons – first, it shows that science rests on a foundation no firmer than that of the religious faiths scientists mock, and, second, it suggests that scientists' thinking processes are far too limited to reach beyond the very narrow confines of a discipline they follow with unquestioning belief.

The point of skeptical nihilism is not to discover, for example, that Albert Einstein and Charles Darwin (or any other highly respected "genius" scientist) are wrong but rather to learn that they are both right, *at best*, only within the narrow confines of a very small "sliver" of reality and that we can, *if we choose*, move "beyond" their theories into much vaster realms beyond the reach of physical science and its instruments. We simply must awaken first from the dream of our current beliefs.

And why not move "beyond" those beliefs in scientific progress if by so doing we are no longer passive participants in physical reality but active creators of a world we *intend* to live in? ***For too long, scientific progress, religion, and modern forms of government have hypnotized us into believing we are capable of far less than we actually are***. But now that we have used skeptical nihilism to break the hypnosis, why not scrap scientific progress forever, replacing it with another set of beliefs that, in effect, hands back to us direct control over our lives?

Our ability to choose our beliefs regardless of what the "evidence" suggests and to make those beliefs effective in our daily lives is far more valuable than mere social traditions like religion, science, and politics. We simply need to reacquaint ourselves with the ability to choose – and that is the purpose of the exercises below.

My message will likely smack of arrogance, elitism, and self-delusion. I don't see any way to avoid that impression, though I certainly don't intend to be arrogant and I'm quite certain I'm not deluding myself. (You'll have to trust me on that.)

I don't mind the charge of elitism, however, because so-called democratic ideals have also been used over the years primarily to keep people asleep. (Democracy and democratic ideals are second only to scientific progress as my favorite "punching bag" of skeptical nihilism. Both are far too widely respected out of ignorant complacency, especially in the United States and Europe.)

So for example, the characteristically American idea that we are "all created equal" entirely glosses over the fact we are all created equally sleeping and therefore all equally in need of being awakened. Once awakened, however, we become part of a "higher" order. So let's be honest here – the awakened ones form a kind of aristocracy in the sense they have a superior ("higher," "transcendent") perspective on humanity compared with the sleepers.

To put this idea into more forceful language: *we are all created (born) equally stupid, but it's an open question whether, as adults, each of us has the intelligence, courage, and commitment to rise above ourselves*. Of course, *if* the majority of us were to rise above the herd, the herd would move up a notch, so to speak. But I don't expect that to happen anytime soon. Indeed, "higher forces" may *never* "allow" it to happen for reasons I will not disclose here. (The final point is for another book.)

So for the time being, "rising above ourselves," i.e., "waking from the dream of our beliefs" is a solitary endeavor pursed by outsiders and lone wolfs. It's important to keep in mind that the project I describe in this book puts you at odds with society (the "herd" or "crowd") and may even make you *appear* anti-social, sociopathic, psychopathic. If being perceived as such disturbs you (and it would disturb many people), you may want to reconsider pursuing this project, as your chances of seeing it through to the end become vanishingly small and you could cause irrevocable damage to your mind and body.

3. ***Why do I believe people should be awakened?***

Asking me why I believe people should be awakened is, I think, another way of asking why I'm publishing this book at all. In any case, I honestly don't know if anyone *should* be awakened. Phrased in that manner, the question is a moral one, and I don't feel I'm in a position to state what anyone should or should not do. But I will say this – everyone should have the *option* to awaken if it so happens life's events work in their favor, making the possibility of awakening a real probability.

The reason I'm publishing this book rather than keeping this information private is that I want to *help* people do something for which there are very few if any real guidelines. My hope is that by reading this book, people will at least begin to *conceive* of the idea of awakening and, beyond that, will be able to use the methods described herein to actually awaken. Whether any of that will come to pass remains to be seen.

I should also acknowledge there's a presumption (or hypothesis) here that a book can help anyone at all. Based solely on my own experience of awakening, I have no good reason to believe reading a book like this, by itself, could trigger an awakening process. I never had such a book at my disposal nor a person who stood in for such a book and offered me regular advice during my own ordeal of awakening. Quite the opposite, in fact. The awakening events I mentioned above "descended" on me, as it were, arriving out of nowhere, unexpected, never summoned (at least consciously). While it's true I did rely on a wide range of literature to help me interpret those events afterwards, I was on my own when they occurred. My hope is that this book can serve to guide someone through the awakening process and in so doing, accelerate the experience, make it more efficient. But there's no way I can guarantee such an outcome.

Briefly, I also want to mention the concept of secrecy. Am I divulging any secrets by publishing this information? Am I breaking an oath? Not really. That's because if there are any secrets here at all, they are quite distinct from, say, state secrets. This information remains a secret only to those who have not put in the effort to try to understand it. However, if you exert yourself and increase your understanding of the material, what once might have seemed like a secret is naturally and unavoidably revealed to you on an internal level, *without the need for human communication*. Compare that situation with a state secret, where a person must communicate the secret to you for you to know it (or you must steal it from them). Thus, while it's possible to hide a state secret indefinitely if sufficient safeguards are in place, it's impossible to hide a "growth secret" forever because fewer safeguards exist the more a person knows.

I also want to discuss whether what I'm publishing here is, in any meaningful sense, dangerous or threatening to anyone. Briefly, yes it's threatening, very threatening – that's the whole point. It's threatening, first of all, to the person who will undertake these exercises, threatening to his ego, his identity, his personality, his deep sleep. Secondly, assuming the person who undertakes these exercises successfully completes them and awakens (a very big assumption, of course), this information becomes threatening to any "authority figures" or "experts" who benefit from ruling over a society of sleepers. As I see it, that would at least include governments, corporations, and universities.

Now, stated in that way, the potential situation seems alternatively dire or ludicrously overstated, and it's probably a little of both. In any case, I doubt there's a reason for anyone to become too anxious in the short term (read: until the end of the current century). I don't foresee a social revolution being triggered by what I've written here because I don't foresee large numbers of people being inspired to put aside their day jobs to pursue these tasks (I'm a true pessimist in that sense). But if my foresight is mistaken, ... well, then it's more than just society that's in for a shock, as this very reality will, in a very *real* sense, be rent asunder – and that's *not* at all bad thing!

Clearly our work is cut out for us: the entire edifice of modern society would seem to resist the task at hand. The common sense of the crowd states that we are "insane" for trying to do what we're setting out to do because we're trying to do the impossible. Scientists state that our task is irrational because it has no empirical evidence, no data whatsoever to back it up. The religious community describes our task as blasphemous because it sounds suspiciously like we're setting ourselves up to be God the Creator. Finally, government leaders and politicians, though typically slow to realize it, may feel threatened by our task because it teaches us to listen to ourselves first and foremost before we consider listening to them.

I hope that last paragraph sounds as ridiculous to the reader as it does to me (which doesn't mean it's false, of course).

4. ***Why are people born sleeping only to remain so for the rest of their lives?***

Whether what I've written above is indeed the case is something each reader has to work out for himself and herself. While, at one extreme, I hope readers don't flat out reject this book as the ravings of a lunatic, at the other extreme, I also hope readers don't merely embrace it as an article of faith. I believe this book should be an inspiration for radical, committed, lifelong work.

As I stated above, the immediate goal of awakening is a totally committed skeptical nihilism that leaves no human belief or piece of knowledge standing in its wake. The two intermediate goals are, first, a direct experience of the "higher" reality that remains when you have awakened and second, the training to cultivate your daily life from the perspective of that higher reality. Finally, the long-term goal (*very* long term) is a society or civilization composed of people who have awakened and now live every moment of their lives in that higher reality. Robotic idol-worship of God or science would have no place in such a society.

In any case, if what I've written does bear out for all or even some readers, one of the first questions on their minds (certainly the first on mine at the time) will be *why is it so? Why are people born sleeping, rarely if ever to awaken from the dream of their beliefs before they die?*

First of all, if that question has an answer, you will not find it *within* this reality since the answer addresses humanity *as a whole* and therefore must exist "outside" humanity. (That's a somewhat technical point but essential to mention.) Secondly, because the answer exists only outside this reality, you will never find it by relying on human pursuits like philosophical reasoning and scientific research. Please carefully consider that point. Finally, I think it's mysterious that we can ask the question at all even though we cannot find its answer here. Why that's so I do not know (though I've speculated on it).

Next, I would like to describe the personality and daily behavior of someone like myself who has devoted their lives to completing these exercises.

First off, I've experienced no indications that awakening causes the human organism to vanish or become modified in some unpredictable way. *Completing these exercises leads to a fundamentally different attitude toward the human organism (and human society) but it does not affect the general appearance or functioning of the human organism.* The laws of biology and physics remain intact, and I offer myself as proof. (You'll have to trust me here. I'm not providing photographs of myself "before" and "after" awakening, but if I did you would note I look the same.)

More importantly, the new attitude leads to a new set of observable behavioral tendencies that can be summed up as *an intensified inner focus during daily life* or, phrased differently, *an increased tendency to favor introspection over acting out and drama.* As a matter of daily practice, someone awakened will turn *inward* to find solutions to life's problems rather than outward toward authority figures and experts. By turning inward, they may directly access and control the feelings and beliefs that condition the world they experience, and by discarding and/or adding to those beliefs, they may directly modify that experience. This inner focus significantly reduces the awakened one's reliance on other people and material things, also reducing the amount of drama in their daily lives.

The reasons for this increased introspective tendency are clear. Because waking from the dream of your beliefs puts you into contact with a "higher" *inner* reality, your attention or awareness is now "split," as it were, between two realities, the higher reality you "discover" using this book's exercises and the lower, human reality you have experienced since birth. The way you access the higher reality is through internal processes like imagination, feeling, contemplation, and meditation.

The more attention and focus you give to the inner reality, the more you appreciate *it is the inner reality, with its beliefs and intentions, that gives rise to the outer reality, not vice versa*. This observation directly contradicts the current scientific belief systems, which hold that matter (the brain and body) gives rise to inner mental activity. In fact, the situation turns out to be the opposite.

Finally, by increasingly identifying yourself with the "higher" reality rather than the lower human reality, you increasingly identify yourself with some "thing" outside of time and space and, by definition, eternal. You come to understand that while your body may die and your personality cease to exist, "you" continue to exist because "you" *are* that higher reality, in some sense, and therefore also eternal. *The goal of this book is to help you find "you,"* to put it cryptically but nonetheless accurately. Only then can you become the sole authority over your own life.

I know I've said a lot in the last few paragraphs, and all will be fleshed out below. But I cannot emphasize enough the importance of this "split attention" or "split awareness," as it is the defining characteristic of anyone completing these exercises. Indeed, this characteristic colors even the most mundane daily decisions of an awakened one, as he or she makes choices no longer based solely on selfish desires and needs but also on the higher "requirements" of the higher reality. While those higher requirements may be interpreted analogously to moral imperatives, they are in fact immaterial "laws" that limit what we can and cannot do as human beings.

Meanwhile, those who have not completed the exercises (i.e., most of humanity) will continue to find their attention focused only on this lower, human reality for the duration of their lives. They either do not suspect or outright deny the existence of a "higher" reality. For them, humanity exists alone, as it were, and is an end in itself. For them, selfishness and existential solitude are natural if unfortunate aspects of human life.

In contrast, from the perspective of someone like myself and others who complete these exercises, humanity exists as a smaller (though very important) part of a much larger or higher reality and therefore may serve as a stepping stone to "higher" things. In other words, *for those who are awakened, humanity becomes a means to an end rather than an end in itself*.

The implications of what I've italicized above are vast and, in some sense, frightening. This is as it should be. On the awakened view, humanity is something to experience fully and then leave behind for "higher pursuits," not something to enjoy as an end in itself. The so-called pleasures of human existence become, at best, a means to advance beyond humanity or, at worst, a long series of distractions and distortions that keep us asleep in the dream of our beliefs.

5. ***Why this book now?****

Also see Appendix C.

I suspect this book is "appearing" now because scientific progress has advanced to a point where humanity has been fully robbed of its inner powers of control. From this book's perspective, first religion and then science have led humanity into a dead end. That's because both have "taught" humanity the lesson (i.e., the unfounded belief) that human beings have no control over the reality they find themselves in and that whatever goes on "in their heads" is just a kind of sideshow to the real thing: manipulating material reality with machines and devices and/or prayers to God.

In contrast to both science and religion, the clear implication of this book's exercises is that *control over daily life originates within you, in your mental, emotional and imaginative activity, in your committed intentions,* and does not require machines or devices or prayer to God. Given the current dominance of scientific and religious thinking in our society, this book's perspective will appear like rank superstition and pseudoscience to most readers, and they will have to struggle mightily to overcome that common sense view along with the fear and laziness underlying it.

Indeed, while the transition from religion to science is touted in history books as "progress" and an improvement of the overall human condition, from this book's perspective the transition did little to relieve humanity's helplessness and lack of control, except that, rather than groveling before God, we now grovel before automobiles, aircraft, computer networks, modern medicine, and other "material conveniences." However, *if we so choose, we may grovel before absolutely nothing* – and "absolutely nothing" is something quite amazing to behold.

Moreover, waking from the dream of your beliefs and realizing you are in control means "it's all on you": *because only you create your reality through your intentions and beliefs, only you are ultimately responsible for your experience of reality*. So if one day you find your property destroyed or your body ravaged by disease or that you've become the victim of some other catastrophe, only you are responsible for the beliefs that caused that situation (not the "evils of society," "bad eating habits" or any other fashionable excuse) and only you can modify your beliefs to rectify the situation (not authority figures like the government or experts like doctors, lawyers, and scientists).

The shocking fact (to me at least) is that we as a civilization have long forgotten how we create and control this universe *from the inside out*, using our beliefs, intentions, and feelings to materialize what we "see" in our imaginations. Our collective thoughts and actions everyday indicate we deny this process occurs and sustains the universe. As a result of that denial, we attempt to control the outer world rather than the inner world and find ourselves in endless personal, professional, and political turmoil. And when we ask ourselves why we can never seem to banish conflict from the world we live in, we erroneously conclude that the answer is a need for still more means of outer control, which only further escalates the turmoil and increases the likelihood of hatred and war.

Ultimately, each us can control only one thing: ourselves, i.e., our own thoughts, feelings and beliefs. And by learning first to control those things within us, we may only then control the world outside of us. *Control yourself first, be your own government, then any world you want is immediately at your fingertips*. Until we collectively understand the italicized sentence, and alter our beliefs about what humanity can do, we will continue to find ourselves in a world where political and social leadership with the best intentions inevitably results in some of the worst possible outcomes.

With that necessary bit of social criticism behind us, we are now ready to begin the exercises.

Part II: Practice

6. *Introduction and Preparations*

Here the task at hand is to do the one thing you most don't *want to do:* ***leave your humanity behind forever***. To have even a fighting chance of succeeding, the reader needs to make proper preparations.

The most basic requirement is a "life pause" to help sustain the self-reflection and self-observation that all of these exercises require. That means *stop whatever it is you are doing right now*, regardless of how much you *believe* you enjoy or benefit from it, and retreat to a quiet, dimly lit room where you are alone, undisturbed, able to sit in a comfortable chair for periods of at least an hour or two. You should also have at your side food and drink (unless you want to fast during this work) and a notebook or tape recorder to leave a record of what transpires. In the notebook, you will record your reflections and observations however you see fit.

This entire set of exercises consists of a series of interior processes that will require your sustained abilities to think logically, to feel deeply, and to imagine clearly. Thus, at the outset we must accept an unavoidable paradox: *we have only our most human qualities of thinking, feeling, and imagination to help us rise above and leave behind our humanity*. Or, to put it slightly differently, ***we must rely on human experience to help us transcend human experience***.

If that paradox does not sit well with you for any reason, if rather than bring a smile to your face it causes consternation and annoyance, please do not proceed further and instead continue to mull over the paradox itself.

Please consider that it is everyday life and common sense we are *intentionally* leaving behind here. Also please consider it's common sense or, more cynically, the "herd mentality" that traps us in our limited notions of what humanity is capable of. And finally consider that by leaving humanity behind and moving forward with these exercises, the reader will become "anti-social" over the duration of the exercises, an outsider, a stranger, perhaps even described as a sociopath. But *right now*

I trust the reader is brave and committed enough not to let mere words block his or her progress.

So, to briefly summarize, the ends or goals of these exercises are (in order):

a. To stabilize one's identity in the higher reality;
b. To split one's awareness between the higher reality and the more familiar human reality;
c. To select the core beliefs that will serve as the basis for your human life moving forward;
d. To get on with your life.

All of those goals except for the final one can be reached sitting alone in a chair in a dimly lit room. So that is what you will regularly do for as long as it takes to complete the tasks.

Also, to summarize, the means to achieving the above goals are (in order):

a. To understand the origin of all your current beliefs;
b. To subject those current beliefs to skeptical nihilism, overturning all belief systems, including common sense;
c. Finally, to recognize yourself as devoid or empty of all beliefs and at the same time in direct contact with a higher reality (which is the first of the goals listed above).

All of those means can be had sitting alone in a comfortable chair in an empty room.

So there you have it, the ends and the means that together comprise this book's exercises. In what follows, I will provide more detail on many of the individual exercises. I do so with some concern, however, because I can only describe the process as I remember experiencing it (and I did keep a thorough notebook at the time). While I hope my personal experience can provide signposts to other readers performing the exercises, I'm also aware I'm running the risk of unduly influencing my readers' experience, which should be unique to them and their respective backgrounds (and it will be unique regardless of whether or not they expect to have an experience identical to mine).

Consequently, please understand the following descriptions as signposts and milestones that will *probably* also mark your experience of the exercises. Nonetheless, I cannot offer any guarantees that events will proceed with readers exactly as they did with me.

7. *The Means*

The initial work – the means to the end – involves systematically reviewing our collective knowledge of daily reality and the universe, creating a finite list of core beliefs that underlie all that knowledge, understanding the origin of those core beliefs, and finally subjecting those core beliefs to a skeptical reasoning process that leads you to abandon them all.

By "core beliefs" I mean those few beliefs that are broad and general enough to logically support all of our knowledge and daily experience. If those core beliefs fall, all other beliefs logically dependent on them will fall as well. In that way, knocking down the core beliefs is sufficient to make rubble of the entire "knowledge edifice," as it were. Only when you have disposed of all beliefs, emptied yourself entirely of knowledge, can you proceed to the second half of the work, "the Ends."

a. Reviewing knowledge and identifying core beliefs

The knowledge review begins by dividing up what we know about the universe into bins that roughly correspond to educational subjects – e.g., physical sciences, engineering, medicine, social sciences, the arts, the humanities, politics, business and finance, jurisprudence, architecture, etc. (This division is purely heuristic, to make the task more manageable.)

Of course, each of those bins contains a huge number of beliefs about the "corner" of reality that particular subject addresses. However, you will find that for each subject, most of its beliefs are logically dependent on a very few "key subject matter beliefs," as I call them. Identify those beliefs for each subject and list them out. The next step is then to go even broader, more general, identifying "core beliefs" that subtend all or most of those key subject matter beliefs. In this context, core beliefs are often "hidden behind" the other beliefs, leading us to forget they exist. Indeed, most of us live our entire lives never enumerating those core beliefs, remaining forever unaware they are implied by our every action.

Nonetheless, as we'll see below, those core beliefs form the "underpinning" or "foundation" of what we call civilization. Without those beliefs, we have no civilization at all, strange as that may sound. And it's for that reason the core beliefs are the focus of these exercises: if we can dispose of those core beliefs with our skeptical nihilism, we will also dispose of civilization.

Reading back over what I wrote above (and despite running it through multiple editorial passes), I see it is all still rather abstract. So below I will provide a list of what I discovered (at the time) to be the necessary and sufficient core beliefs of Western Civilization. As far as I know, no one has ever published such a list before.

To repeat, these are the core beliefs (presented as simple assertions) that provide the basis on which we have built the current "scientifically minded" civilization. Pretty much anyone you meet on the street would consider these core beliefs as "common sense" (certainly all trained scientists would) and therefore not worthy of skepticism. However, they are precisely the target of our skepticism in these exercises, as our goal is to "escape" from their influence and reach a higher, richer, wider reality.

The core beliefs of Western Civilization are:

<u>Core beliefs about reality:</u>

1) The reality of my five senses is all that exists;
2) The reality of my five senses exists in space and in time;
3) The reality of my five senses is governed only by random physical and chemical forces;
4) The reality of my five senses is not directly influenced by thoughts, feelings, and intentions;

<u>Core beliefs about humanity:</u>

5) I am a biological organism composed of random physical and chemical forces;
6) My five senses cannot operate outside of space and time;

7) My five senses are insufficient by themselves to detect and measure the physical and chemical forces that govern reality;
8) My thoughts, feelings, and intentions cannot directly influence the biological processes of which I am composed;

   Core beliefs about core beliefs:
9) The above eight core beliefs are "true" because they are supported by scientific (empirical) evidence;
10) Anyone who doesn't seriously believe the above eight core beliefs is either insane (in some sense of that word), a genuine fool, or, at best, pulling our leg and should not be taken at their word.

So there you have it – the necessary and sufficient core beliefs of our scientifically minded civilization. You may generate a different list of core beliefs, of course, but this is the list I originally developed. Try as I might, over the last 15 years I have never been able to add or take away from this list without introducing redundancies or leaving something important out. For that reason I describe it as necessary and sufficient.

Please note how each of the first eight core beliefs imposes implicit limitations on humanity. Appreciating this point is critical before proceeding with the exercises, for it is these very limitations we strive to overcome.

For example, core belief 5 requires us to be organisms without a soul or spirit; core belief 6 rules out clairvoyance and telepathy; core belief 7 requires us to use instruments like telescopes, microscopes, and cyclotrons to understand how the universe works rather than our naked senses or internal processes like meditation; core belief 8 requires us to use material medicines and rules out healing by the mind.

I'll leave it to the reader as an exercise to work through all the implied limitations. There are a lot more human activities ruled out by the core beliefs, and they would all be filed by physical scientists under categories like "pseudoscience," "superstition," "the supernatural," or "the occult." The implication, obviously, is that if it's ruled out by the core set of beliefs listed above, it's not a legitimate intellectual pursuit and deserves only scorn from the scientific and medical "experts," who will tell you those "other" activities have no evidence to support them.

That brings me to the final two beliefs on the list, which are meta-beliefs, "core beliefs about core beliefs." Those two beliefs are critical for maintaining the integrity of the list but they are also the weakest points of the list and most susceptible to skeptical nihilism.

Meta-belief 9 serves to delimit what counts as support for "justified true belief" in our scientifically minded civilization – namely, scientific evidence, i.e., evidence detectable and measurable by a scientific instrument. To clearly draw out what is packed into this particular meta-belief, we can rephrase it as "a core belief is true if and only if it is supported by scientific evidence detectable by scientific instruments, which are our only true means of measuring reality."

Clearly, then, a major assumption is hidden in meta-belief 9: only scientific instruments can tell us the truth about the world we live in. Moreover, unlike the previous eight core beliefs, this meta-belief cannot be founded on scientific evidence without setting up a tautology. Therefore, it is a purely arbitrary belief no different from an expanded belief such as "both scientific and non-scientific instruments can tell us the truth about the world we live in" (where non-scientific instruments refer to our naked, unaided senses, for example, or to our imagination).

In any case, it is this unfounded hidden assumption in meta-belief 9 that is its ultimate undoing as well as the undoing of the entire list of core beliefs. For once we adopt a different set of core beliefs that allow many non-scientific routes to reality (and nothing is preventing us from allowing that), we open up a vast field of endeavors that include all of the occult and pseudoscience activities previously denigrated by physical scientists as false and deceptive.

Turning now to meta-belief 10, we see that it serves to uphold the sanctity of the other core beliefs, as it were. Based solely on that belief about core beliefs, this book I am writing must be considered the work of a fool, a joker, or a lunatic – period. There are no other options because this book doesn't presume the truth of the first eight core beliefs (that's the whole point of waking from the dream of our beliefs, after all) and therefore this book must, in that sense, be completely "wrong" or, at best, be a work of the highly suspicious occult or supernatural variety (which it most definitely is, by the way).

b. *Identifying the social origin of core beliefs*

So now that the core beliefs of civilization are out in the open, we can assault them with our skeptical nihilism and reduce them all to disposable, relative truths. The nihilistic process works as follows. (Please don't take my word for this series of intellectual "discoveries" – each person must work this out for himself and herself.)

The reasoning proceeds as follows.

Each of the ten core beliefs listed above must originate or come from somewhere; we were not born programmed with those beliefs as stated in English or any other language. So where did we get them? Well, skeptical introspection reveals we learned each of the core beliefs (or, more cynically, were persuaded of them) from authority figures, our parents and teachers, who taught us everything we "know" about how to behave, live, and function in society. True, no one literally handed us a list of core beliefs and said, "Believe this, son and daughter; to function in our civilization, you must take these core beliefs to heart, otherwise you'll be considered weird and insane." Nonetheless, our subsequent development into adults is *as if* we were handed just such a list and given just such direction, and that point is sufficient for this argument to stand. Please consider the last comment deeply.

Going on: but if we inherited our core beliefs from parents and teachers, and they themselves from their own parents and teachers, then those core beliefs first of all and *perhaps only* reflect an educational tradition marked by a specific time and place, just as all historical traditions are so marked.

Still further: and if indeed the core beliefs are only a historical tradition, then they are, at best, true relative only to a specific time, place, and society, for how could they be universally true unless they, in some manner, entered our world untouched by history, which does not seem to be the case.

And further: but if those core beliefs are only specific to a narrow range of time and place, it's reasonable and logical to propose that the core beliefs listed above might never have existed at all, or have existed in an entirely different form, had their society of origin never existed or existed in an entirely different form from our current society.

Thus, we arrive at the basic conclusion that *our core beliefs about reality and life are true relative only to the traditions of a specific civilization that might just as well have never existed or have existed in a radically altered form.*

Now, the reader may or may not agree with that conclusion, but in any case, he should make clear to himself exactly where in the above line of reasoning he falls out of agreement – and right there is where he will find a resistance point to overcome.

But let's move on: first, I'm certainly not the first person to develop such an argument and arrive at the nihilistic conclusion I italicized above. For example, most trained anthropologists would agree with the conclusion (though they wouldn't call themselves nihilists). But, as I said before, here the difference is what I will *do* with that conclusion. I will use it as a basis by which to awaken from the dream of my beliefs and rise above humanity. And to help me do that, I will require an additional tool beyond my skeptical reasoning power – my imagination.

But before I continue on, I want to go on a bit of a tangent and address the one group of people who, I'm certain, will strenuously disagree with the above conclusion: physical scientists, i.e., physicists, chemists, biologists, geologists, and also most clinicians. They will flat out disagree with the conclusion regardless of what argument led to it. That's because it's inconceivable to them that cells, molecules, atoms, and subatomic particles are all, at most, concepts that resulted from a social educational process and therefore "exist" only relative to the historical traditions of the civilization where that education occurred (i.e., Western civilization).

Indeed, the resistance to the above conclusion spreads far beyond physical scientists to include most anyone who considers themselves educated. For all those people, the core beliefs listed above would be considered common sense, the results of scientific progress, and a reasonably accurate reflection of an objective reality – all because (in a circularly logical fashion) those beliefs are supported by empirical evidence.

Yet, to honestly state that point of view, the physicist must deny that everything he knows about physics – the theories, the hypotheses, the methods and techniques used to gather data to test those theories and hypotheses – he necessarily learned from someone else, taking them at their word, following their instructions, training himself to become an independent physicist who can add to the physics knowledge base if he follows the proper protocols.

Moreover, the entire edifice of physics training and education might just as well not exist or exist in an entirely different form, and if it did exist in a different form, the science of physics would be entirely different, with a different set of theoretical constructs, a different set of techniques to gather data, a different set of criteria for what counts as "good data." As a result, the physicist would have an entirely different view of what processes and objects constitute physical reality compared with what we now consider true of objective reality – and, most importantly, no one would have any criteria to decide which form of physics is the "right" or "true" form without committing logical errors like begging the question.

Thus, we are led to back to the earlier conclusion: *our core beliefs about reality and life (including our physical and chemical theories) are true relative only to the traditions of a specific civilization that might just as well have never existed or have existed in a radically altered form.*

In fact, what's happening in society today reflects very poorly on scientific progress and illustrates the sort of herd mentality this book's exercises are designed to eradicate: first, physical scientists acquire their training and theoretical constructs; second, those scientists conveniently "forget" or "deny" that everything they so acquired was transmitted to them by fallible human beings; third, also without apparently realizing it, they project those theoretical constructs onto the reality they perceive, *creating* an objective reality; fourth, they set up experiments whose design presupposes the existence of those theoretical constructs; fifth, based on the results of those experiments, they proclaim either the existence or nonexistence of the theoretical construct; and sixth, all the non-scientists in society take those physicists at their word because, after all, they are "experts" on the laws of the universe.

By the way, I'm not picking on physicists here. The same process occurs with chemistry, biology, geology, meteorology, medicine, and some other fields where "expertise" exists. The reader is encouraged to work those out for himself.

I've gone to some lengths fleshing out this argument relative to the physical sciences because I am certain there will be more resistance to this book from that quarter than from anywhere else. And yet it's not like they have never heard this argument – I know many of them have heard it, as I have presented it to them, and their response is typically a wordless, blank stare before returning to their research. It's inconceivable to them that all of their research and theories, supported as they are by so much high quality data, could all nonetheless amount to nothing more than a shaggy dog story that has no more basis in reality than a piece of science fiction.

Of course, my hope is that the argument here has enough force to change behavior – that is, to inspire practicing physical scientists to abandon their scientific research for other pursuits and to encourage nonscientists to respect the opinions of scientific experts much less than they seem to. (Of course, I'm not naïve enough to believe those behavioral changes will happen overnight.)

c. *Rising above all possible core belief systems*

So what have we accomplished so far? Briefly, first we isolated the few core beliefs that underlie all aspects of the current civilization and second, using the method of skeptical nihilism, we showed how each of those beliefs derives from and is sustained by social traditions that might just as well not exist at all.

The realization that the core beliefs exist not because they correspond to an objective reality but because they are merely favored by a social tradition leaves us now (in our minds) with the option of discarding them altogether. And where does that leave "us"? Well, we are left in a state quite literally outside of civilization, even if only in our minds.

The next step is to remain in that state and while there to use our imagination to envision alternate civilizations with alternate core belief systems. In one sense, this part of the exercise is much like imagining various science fiction scenarios. While that might sound like little more than idle daydreaming, the exercise's purpose is to reject each of those imagined belief systems, with the ultimate goal of leaving your mind completely empty of all possible belief systems, a sort of blank slate or tabula rasa.

When you reach the tabula rasa state, you will note that two possible choices confront "you": first, you may act as the arbitrary "creator" of any core belief system and its accompanying civilization, and second, you have the separate option of choosing to create nothing at all and simply acting as a transcendental "observer" of all possible belief systems.

In either of those capacities, whether as a creator or an observer, you have risen above, as it were, all human belief systems and human knowledge, even above systems of language and numbers, above biological and psychological processes. *You have truly emptied out your mind – yet you remain aware and alert and continue to have a sense of identity.* That *feeling* of identity *is* the direct experience of a higher reality.

Now, I've encapsulated a tremendous amount of interior work in just a few paragraphs, and reading back over those paragraphs, I'm concerned a reader might come away from those descriptions thinking the task is little more than a couple afternoons spent daydreaming. But nothing could be further from the truth.

Finding that state of identity with a higher reality, feeling it, then sustaining it over time takes a tremendous amount of concerted effort, and it's very subtle work. While I'm convinced anyone can do it if he or she is sufficiently committed, the reader should be careful not to underestimate the challenges. After all, up until now, readers will have spent their entire lives cramming knowledge and belief into their minds, and now they are being asked to clear all of that material out and, moreover, to experience the very subtle "residue" that remains. That residue, in fact, is your first glimpse of a higher, more expansive reality, far more inclusive of existential possibilities than the daily reality you've experienced since birth.

The second half of the exercises – what I have called "The Ends" – are devoted to learning about that higher reality and ultimately getting you as familiar with its terrain as you are with the terrain of daily life.

To help the reader still better understand what is required of the methods of skeptical nihilism, I have broken the entire process down into a number of discrete steps listed in **Appendix A**. I intend that list to become a reference for all readers as they master this process. So please refer to it right now and then later as needed.

Before proceeding, I want to emphasize that we've seen the real value of skeptical nihilism in this chapter. We have used its attitudes and arguments to tear down an old, confining core belief system and clear out a space for a new core belief system, which we will develop using exercises in the second half of this book. That process of tearing down and clearing out is itself what I mean by "waking from the dream of our beliefs." And while none of the relativistic reasoning used in this chapter is new or unique to this book, this is the first time, so far as I know, anyone has used this sort of reasoning as a means to a higher end rather than as a logical parlor trick ending in exclamations like "Well, there you have it – everything is relatively true – there are no absolutes – anything goes."

By clearing out a space beforehand, we can be much more confident that our new set of core beliefs, along with the new civilization they imply, will be founded on a firmer, more logically secure basis than if they had been, in some manner, added to the current set of core beliefs listed above. And that, ultimately, is the real value of skeptical nihilism – to clear out a space and prepare for our entrance into a higher reality.

8. *The Ends*

Let's set the stage for the second half of the exercises. So far, we've relied on skeptical nihilism to demonstrate the relative truth, first, of the set of core beliefs underlying our current civilization and, second, of all other possible sets of core beliefs that could underlie any number of alternative civilizations. With that demonstration complete, we are left "observing" (with our mind's eye) an entire array of core belief systems and their implied social arrangements. In other words, as an observer, ***"we" have managed to step outside all possible belief systems and now may view them from a "higher reality." We have thus "awakened from the dream of our beliefs"*** and achieved one of the main goals of these exercises.

There are a few key points we must appreciate about this situation before we proceed to "The Ends."

First, ***having awakened from the dream of our beliefs, our sense of identity has completely transformed itself.*** That transformation occurs because, as "observers," "we" have stepped outside the core belief system of our current civilization, which provided the context for our previous identity based on our mind, body, and personality. Having awakened, we now *recognize* we are identified with a nonphysical, nonhuman feeling or awareness that pervades the higher reality. We thus no longer require a physical or material substrate to support our identity. *"We" have become, in a real sense, nonhuman*. I place the pronoun in quotation marks – "we" – to indicate that new sense of identity.

Second, ***having transformed our identity into a nonphysical point of awareness, we have the privilege of surveying all possible core belief systems and noting their intrinsic limitations***. This is a critical insight because it *reveals* to "us" that, no matter what set of core beliefs we choose to live under and understand the world by, we are imposing physical limits on our nonphysical identity, locking ourselves into a human prison or, to change the metaphor, subjecting ourselves to a dream or delusion.

Further expanding on the second point, ***"we" recognize that all possible core belief systems are equivalent in the sense they must come with physical limitations and thus cannot be absolute in any sense***. None of them can be absolutely true or false, absolutely right or wrong, absolutely good or evil, much like a dream or a delusion can be none of those things.

Indeed, those sorts of dualistic categories are themselves aspects of the very limitations we observe. Thus, if, as human beings, we insist on our core belief system (and its implied civilization) as being "the best developed" or "most advanced," we can do so only arbitrarily and by reference only to social conventions and historical traditions that might just as well have developed differently or not developed at all.

With this second point, we again see the rich fruits of skeptical nihilism.

This brings us to the third point, perhaps the central *practical* point of the whole book: ***"we" recognize we have the ability to choose any core belief system as the basis of our human worldview.*** That is to say, while identified as a nonphysical point of awareness, "we" have a "control point" or, as I like to call it, a "choice function," whereby we may select the set of core beliefs we will live under as a human being. Obviously, given the fruits of skeptical nihilism, that choice can be made based on any criteria of "our" choosing or on no criteria at all.

Please note *it's this nonphysical control point we have completely forgotten about (or deny the existence of) in our current scientifically minded civilization*. And that's because, as something nonphysical and nonmaterial, the control point is undetectable by physical scientific instruments, so there can never be any scientific evidence of its existence. In other words, the prisons of scientific progress and common sense continue to prevent the current civilization from "seeing" the control point and "reaching" it. The whole purpose of these exercises, obviously, is to offer at least one way we may be able to regain that control point (and even then it won't be an easy task).

Now that "we" have identified ourselves as nonphysical points of awareness, we have the privilege of reinventing human civilization, as it were. And we will do that below with a new set of core beliefs.

First, however, we must stabilize our identities in the higher reality while maintaining contact with human reality. Having thus achieved a stabilized identity, we will then begin building a new set of core beliefs that offer a real alternative to the core beliefs of our current scientifically minded civilization. Finally, once we have built that new core set of beliefs, "we" will arbitrarily choose to live by it, becoming examples to our fellow man and woman of how much more "we" can be if we aim higher than mere civilization.

a. Stabilizing our identity in the higher reality

This part of the work continues with regular sessions spent in a comfortable chair and dimly lit room. However, those interior sessions will alternate now with "exterior work," i.e., going out into the bustle of daily life. The goal here is to stabilize our contact with the "higher reality" where our transformed identity exists even while we do all the so-called normal things "sleeping" human beings do, like hold down a job and raise a family.

If we had wanted only to train ourselves to reach a higher reality and then remain there, we would be done now and this book would end. But, I ask you, where's the value in that? I'm not interested in training highly intelligent, committed people to become schizophrenics or shut-ins. My hope is we can directly transform society as a result of having transformed ourselves. For that to happen, we must, at some point, "come down from our mountain" and resume daily life.

The challenge is not falling back into a slumber when we come down from our mountain but remaining alert, awake, and aware, still identified with the "higher reality." In a manner of speaking, we must carry the higher reality around with us, have it hovering over our shoulders as we go about our daily business. I know from personal experience we will require much patience and persistence to achieve this goal because it's so easy to fall back asleep (i.e., get distracted) in civilization.

There is not a lot to write about this stage of the practice because we are not sorting through beliefs or perceptions or any other "things" that we can describe here. Instead, we are focused on focusing, as it were – specifically, focusing on the *feeling* of the higher reality wherever and whenever we "are." It's the same feeling *by definition* that we discovered and "tasted" earlier in the practice. Now it's our task to sustain that feeling over wider and wider stretches of space and time.

So what will we *do* exactly? When we are indoors, we'll sit in the chair in the dimly lit room and force everything out of our mind, especially bodily sensations, until we find the feeling of the higher reality, however faint and transitory, the nonphysical point of awareness with which we now identify. When we "recognize" the feeling again, we will "catch" it, "hold" it, each time for a little while longer. After we're able to hold it over a few minutes, we start trying to hold it while doing increasingly more complex activities – first standing up and moving around the dimly lit room, but soon going into other parts of our residence and then, eventually, going outdoors into rural and urban spaces, always trying to keep the feeling of the higher reality with us.

Over time – weeks, months, perhaps years – we will split our waking awareness into two distinct parts. Strange as that may sound now, it will seem entirely natural once we achieve it. As a result of that split, part of our attention throughout our waking day (as well as during sleep) will *always* be focused on the higher reality. We will always be aware, in other words, that all of our mundane human activities occur in the context of a higher reality that, in a very real sense, determines the very structure of human reality.

When that split awareness is fully established and stabilized, we are ready for the next stage, "The Ends." And by the way, as we progress with this part of the exercise, our friends and colleagues may remark that we seem increasingly serene and detached from life even while we become more effective at achieving our personal and professional goals. In other words, *the more we "pull" the higher reality into the lower reality, the more effective we become in the lower reality even while we care less and less about it.*

So you see how in this particular situation, an increased apathy toward human reality and humanity in general is not necessarily a bad thing and is, in fact, one indication we are making progress with these exercises.

b. Building a new set of core beliefs

Having established a split awareness between the higher reality of our nonphysical point of awareness and the lower reality of our human body, mind, and personality, we are now ready – *if we so choose* – to design and implement a new set of core beliefs.

We also have the option – *if we so choose* – of accepting the set of core beliefs of the current civilization and just going about our daily business with the knowledge that it's all a dream, so to speak.

Please note that either of those options puts us in a higher "aristocracy of being" than the crowds of people who continue to live in the dream of their beliefs as if those beliefs were, in some absolute or objective sense, a reflection of a "true" reality.

In this book, we will explore only the first option: creating a new set of core beliefs as a foundation for a new kind of life, a superior alternative to the current scientifically minded civilization. I may explore the second option in another book or perhaps never at all. By the way, I initially chose the second option myself, the "jaundiced eye" option as I call it, living under its sway for awhile. Though I learned a lot, I eventually felt limited by the jaundiced eye perspective and therefore developed a new set of core beliefs on which to found a new worldview, which I describe here.

So let's focus on generating a new set of core beliefs. Now, because we would prefer that the new set of core beliefs be as internally consistent and certain as possible, we first ask ourselves whether it's possible to design a set of core beliefs capable of withstanding the assault of skeptical nihilism. In other words, can we identify core beliefs that forever exist beyond the pale of skeptical doubt, beliefs that are, in some sense, more robust to skepticism than the beliefs we demolished earlier in the book?

As students of philosophy know, that type of question bedeviled French philosopher Rene Descartes and led him to write his Meditations on First Philosophy, which are often considered the founding documents of the Western philosophical tradition. Since this is not a work of history, I will not recount Descartes' findings. But I will present here (and in Appendix B) my own version of the Cartesian doubting process, which led me to four core beliefs that *do* withstand the assault of skeptical nihilism. Those four core beliefs will form the foundation on which I build the new set of core beliefs that uphold a new worldview.

Please refer to Appendix B for the details of my own Cartesian doubting process. Here I will present only the four core beliefs that result from it (beliefs 1 -4 below).

So here we have it – a new set of core beliefs that support of a new "form" of life:

Core beliefs about humanity (the lower reality):

1) The five, unaided senses are sufficient to define the outer world of human beings;
2) Within the outer world, human beings must occupy a perspective at all times;
3) Human beings also have access to an inner world ("the imagination");
4) In human society, the outer and inner worlds are both linked to language systems.

Core beliefs about nonphysical awareness (the higher reality):

5) "We" are a nonphysical, eternal point of awareness;
6) In the higher reality, "we" occupy a point of control over the lower reality;
7) As the control point, "we" may *choose* core beliefs in accordance with a vision (in the higher reality) that we *intend* to make "real" (in the lower reality);
8) In making that choice, "we" become responsible for whatever human experiences result in the lower reality;
9) By making a series of such choices, "we" may expand our awareness of the diversity of human experience and thus "learn" about humanity.

Core beliefs about core beliefs (meta-beliefs):

10) Core beliefs delimit the scope of all possible human experience;
11) Without core beliefs, human experience does not exist.

The first four core beliefs are necessary and sufficient to define the "lower reality," i.e., the reality where the human organism acts and thinks. As I mentioned above and describe in detail in Appendix B, those four beliefs are necessary and sufficient, on my view, because they withstand the assault of skeptical nihilism: they remain "standing" even after every other possible human belief and activity has been called into doubt, including the activity of skeptical nihilism itself.

By the way, the fact the first four core beliefs withstand skeptical nihilism does not constitute the only reason or even a reason to accept them as core beliefs. After all, one could accept them based on a simple act of recognition or on no basis at all beyond an arbitrary whim – such is the nature of the "choice function" inherent to the higher reality.

Core beliefs 5 through 9 are the centerpiece of this book. They are the core beliefs that became "visible" to "me," so to speak, only *after* I had used skeptical nihilism to demolish the core beliefs of scientifically minded civilization. In other words, the activities and beliefs of civilization had obscured, indeed, had blocked from view, the core beliefs describing a higher reality. I now realize, of course, those core beliefs had existed all along, but I hadn't recognized them owing to my distraction by the supposedly important things happening in civilization. By the way, it is in this very concrete sense that Eastern religions often speak of "Maya" and "samsara" as obscurations that distracts one's attention from enlightenment.

There are many things we could discuss about core beliefs 5 through 9, and I want to touch on a few of their more important aspects right here.

First and foremost, please note that I introduce the first-person pronoun "we" only with the introduction of the core beliefs describing the higher reality. That's because ***"we" are first nonphysical points of awareness that may choose secondarily to undergo a human experience – i.e., we are not human beings first.*** "Our" identity, then, is located *forever* in the higher reality, not in the lower reality where the human organism exists. And if we do choose a human experience, we will *unavoidably* be at the mercy, so to speak, of core beliefs 1 through 4 (and only those beliefs, not one more, not one less).

Secondly, please note that core beliefs 5 through 9 do not and cannot (by definition) have a shred of scientific evidence supporting them. Indeed, "scientific evidence" does not even enter into this new set of core beliefs. Not surprisingly, then, anyone still dreaming under the influence of the core beliefs of scientifically minded civilization will describe core beliefs 5 through 9 as variously "wrong," "false," "completely unsubstantiated," "irrational," "delusional," "crazy," etc.

Thirdly, "our" control point or choice function exists in the higher reality, not in the lower. In other words, freewill exists in the higher reality, not in the lower. Despite making choices every day of its life, the human organism does not enjoy freewill in the same sense the higher nonphysical point of awareness does.

Fourth, the nonphysical point of awareness may enter, exit and reenter human experience as many times as it so chooses. This process we might call "reincarnation." The tendency to choose the same human experience over and over again (regardless of the "reason"), we might call "karma." The opposite tendency of choosing a series of widely different human experiences we might call "consciousness expansion." Indeed, the intentional exploration of a wide variety human experiences could itself comprise a science of sorts, though one quite different in its structure and assumptions from physical science.

Fifth, "truth" does not enter into any of these core beliefs and therefore does not provide a criterion for choosing or not choosing a certain kind of human experience. The "control point," after all, exists in a higher reality untouched by dualistic categories like "true versus false" and "good versus evil."

Conclusion

It's worth mentioning the tremendous amount of pessimism and inaction I've had to overcome to complete this book. The pessimism arises from my limiting belief that the book's message will be *unavoidably* lost on most readers because the message is unavoidably opposed to "common sense," that basic body of knowledge we inherit from our parents and teachers and use throughout our lives to bring sense and safety to what, we believe, would otherwise be a chaotic and confusing world.

Common sense, in other words, is humanity's and civilization's security blanket, and when we remove it from their heads, humanity suddenly feels vulnerable to all the threats they imagine lurk in a world where common sense is absent and everything is permitted.

All that's to say, because this book's message intentionally opposes common sense, it might frighten away readers rather than capture their attention and inspire them to live differently.

In fact, common sense may or may not bolster our security and safety, but one thing this book makes clear: *common sense places narrow limits on what we as human beings believe we are capable of*. In that sense, common sense is a prison, and if you've been in prison long enough, you may begin to interpret your imprisonment as protection against the outside world rather than unjust exclusion from it. Indeed, I believe that's where humanity finds itself today: we mistake our imprisonment in common sense for a form of existential security.

So is there no way out – has common sense trapped us, imprisoned us totally in our human limitations? The reader may not realize it yet, but this book proves the answer to that question is *no*. And while that may sound hopeful, you must face the additional fact that, in any case, you will have to learn from a stranger (this author) if you want to overcome those limitations. *And so I ask you: do you have the courage and commitment to learn from me?*

Appendix A. Summary of the Method of Skeptical Nihilism

According to the method of skeptical nihilism, *we must let go of everything we have ever learned and then recognize where "we" end up.* That includes freeing ourselves from all beliefs, habits, and perceptions, even all relationships and possessions. Unlike other human pursuits, this pursuit is designed to lead us *outside* humanity and civilization, into a higher, nonhuman, nonphysical world that offers a transcendental perspective onto all possible human worlds.

The method of skeptical nihilism may be divided into the following sequence. Here I describe the process as a list of commands to the reader, directing him or her to make increasingly skeptical recognitions about the nature of human reality:

1) Of each theory, belief, opinion, and habit, recognize its origin in human history, note *who* created it, *when* it was created, and *where* (in what social-geographic milieu).

2) Recognize how each belief and habit is unique to a particular place and time, unavoidably limited by history and locale, and therefore necessarily lacking in any universal qualities.

3) Recognize how each belief and habit may or may not have existed, and therefore may or may not be true or false. With this recognition, you overcome the compulsion to truth.

4) Recognize how no belief or habit is any more deserving of your respect and admiration than any other. Nor is any belief or habit any more deserving of your hatred and disgust. With this recognition, you overcome the compulsion to pride.

5) Recognize how, in the previous four steps, you have cut through all habits, traditions, theories and ideologies, all forms of human knowledge – *until finally, paradoxically, all that is left is to cut through skeptical nihilism itself*. Having done that, recognize how detached you feel from each belief and habit. Recognize your lack of desire to cherish any belief or maintain any habit. With these recognitions, you overcome the compulsion to pleasure.

6) Recognize how your total detachment from beliefs and habits *is* **a state of awareness devoid of fear, hope, and desire**. *"You" are no longer you* yet "you" are aware. This awareness exists *outside* the immediate world of our senses. It is a perspective onto our

collective beliefs and habits, the components of all possible civilizations.

7) This imperceptible and indescribable state of awareness *is* **compassionate wisdom** (the author asserts). "You" may remain suspended here indefinitely as a silent "observer" or you may return to daily life or you may continue to expand your awareness into still higher interior realities.

The method of skeptical nihilism works entirely on the reader's internal states, i.e., on his or her thoughts, feelings, beliefs, and intentions. As such, it is practiced in solitude and silence, lying down or sitting, much like more familiar forms of meditation and yoga.

The importance of *recognition* to this overall process should be readily apparent and must be deeply appreciated at all times. By virtue of the goal – a higher reality – we cannot rely on tools of the lower, human reality such as logical reasoning and scientific instrumentation. We may rely only on our interior states to recognize what is happening. The constant risk here of self-deception and self-delusion should be obvious. Please be aware!

Appendix B. Skeptical Nihilism Applied To Human Experience

Here I describe the results of applying the method of skeptical nihilism to human experience. What I uncover are *the four fundamental "features" of human experience*, which exist under any metaphysical circumstance, as it were, and are thus impervious to all forms of doubt, skepticism, and deception.

This application of skeptical nihilism is actually an updated version of Rene Descartes' program of comprehensive doubt described in his Meditations on First Philosophy. Like the Cartesian program, the purpose of my application of skeptical nihilism is to identify a set of *certain assertions* about human experience (or *features*, as I call them) that become the foundation on which to build a new set of core beliefs for a "new" form of life (as described in the second half of this book).

The four fundamental features described below are what "remain" after we apply skeptical nihilism to all human knowledge and experience, including, most importantly, applying skeptical nihilism to itself (described in Step 5 of Appendix A). It's worth noting that Descartes makes the analogous maneuver in his analysis when he applies doubt to itself (i.e., when he doubts doubt) only to discover that thought "remains." Based on that outcome, he makes his famous statement, "I think therefore I am," where the word "therefore" (*ergo*) is properly interpreted as an act of intuition or recognition, not as a logical consequence.

Thus, for both Descartes' and my program, what "remains" as certain beyond a doubt must be recognized or intuited as such. In his case, it is "thought" that's intuited. In my case, it's the four fundamental features that are intuited. As the reader will see below, what Descartes calls "thought" overlaps with the four fundamental features I "discovered" using skeptical nihilism.

While only an act of recognition or intuition will take us definitively "beyond" doubt, I believe additional support for the certainty of a feature of human experience can be found in arguments that derive a contradiction from assuming that a feature is *not* certain. The reader may or may not be persuaded by those arguments, but for the sake of comprehensiveness I present them below for each of the four features where such arguments are applicable.

Feature 1: **The immediate world defined by our five senses**. While all manner of uncertainties and errors may (and do) occur *within* the immediate world of our five senses, the existence of that world *as a whole* is certain. That world is "immediate" because it is the "first thing" that confronts us every instant, providing the "content" of our lives. All human disputes and conflicts must occur *within* the immediate world of our five senses.

We cannot believe the immediate world of our five senses "does not exist," for in so speaking or believing we unavoidably invoke that world's existence. Thus, while we may deny the existence of any particular thing within the immediate world of our senses, we cannot deny the existence of that world *as a whole* without contradicting ourselves.

Nor can we believe the immediate world of our senses "is an illusion" or "is false," for that would imply a comparison of the immediate world of our senses to another "true" world undistorted by our senses. Yet, even if such a "true" world existed, how could we make such a comparison without relying on our senses and potentially introducing distortions? Thus, while we may believe particular perceptions to be illusory or false, we cannot believe the immediate world of our five senses *as a whole* is illusory or false. We must withhold belief on whether that's the case.

Feature 2: **The perspective within the immediate world of our senses**. All human perception originates from a body located at a particular place (culture) and time (history). We therefore learn about and analyze the world of our senses from a particular perspective. Given the infinite nature of space and time, the number of possible perspectives within that world is presumably also infinite.

Feature 3: **The imagination that envisions variations in the world of our five senses even when those variations are imperceptible.**

Feature 4: **The spoken language that describes the world of our five senses and imagination**. Following social convention, we say that a particular description is "true" if the evidence justifies our belief in that description. The totality of descriptions is our *knowledge* of the immediate world of our five senses (what philosophers call "discursive knowledge").

The above *4 features* are summarized by stating the following: **Each human being perceives, imagines and learns to speak about the world from his or her unique perspective**. We may call that statement the *fundamental limitation on humanity.* If the reader has any difficulties accepting that statement and the unavoidable limitations it implies, he or she should go back and reread the *4 features* to determine exactly where the misunderstandings lie.

Below I analyze the *unavoidable social implications* of the fundamental limitation on humanity:

1) "A *unique* perspective": because each time and place is logically excluded from all other times and places, each perspective is singular and unique. Therefore, an unavoidable multiplicity of perspectives *must* exist in society.

2) "A unique *perspective*": every belief, theory, or ideology is unavoidably colored by the perspective of the person creating it and therefore *cannot* apply to society as a whole, without society first being *persuaded* of its universal applicability – and persuasion, by definition, relies on force and charisma, not on a logically consistent argument.

3) "Each human being *perceives, ...*": Our perceptions of society – sight, hearing, touch, taste, smell – are unavoidably colored by our perspective.

4) "Each human being ... *imagines, ...*": What we imagine about society, based as it is on our perceptions, is unavoidably colored by our perspective.

5) "Each human being ... *learns to speak ...*": All social discourse is unavoidably determined by a language we *must* learn from our parents and teachers. Therefore, every claim we make about what we perceive and imagine (i.e., our knowledge) is unavoidably limited by a language we inherited from society. While we, as individuals, may change that language at our will, those changes may not apply to the language as a whole, without other speakers first being *persuaded* of their universal applicability.

A summary statement of the social implications: **The unavoidable historical and geographical limitations of our individual perspectives result in unavoidable limitations on our knowledge and understanding of the world and make a universal perspective impossible *within* the world of our senses.**

If a universal or absolute perspective (or description) existed *within* the immediate world of our senses, it would have to prove how it encompasses all other perspectives and descriptions. Yet how could it prove that without using criteria unavoidably colored by its own perspective? Thus, it is impossible to prove that any one perspective within the world of our senses is universal without committing the logical error of begging the question.

Thus, given only the evidence of our senses, we must remain agnostic on the existence or non-existence of an absolute or universal perspective -- i.e., we cannot have knowledge of (i.e., cannot detect or measure) such a perspective.

Therefore, when we believe and act upon knowledge, as we do in everyday life, we do so relative to particular (limited) knowledge, not relative to absolute or universal knowledge.

Appendix C. Why Nihilism Now?

Throughout history we find authority figures and experts supporting and even celebrating humanity's limitations in the name of progress. Never do we find those same figures encouraging their fellow men and women to transcend those limitations, to become something "higher" than a mere human being and, in the process, become one's own authority and expert on one's own existence. As a result, society after society and civilization after civilization remain mired in a lower, biological reality, bogged down in conceptual limitations and ignorance that masquerade as common sense and progress.

We need nihilism now to help us abolish those limitations and transform ourselves into a higher form of life that rules by its own, innate authority and expertise.

The situation we find ourselves in today is not, on the face of it, surprising. We were raised by authority figures (our parents and teachers) who, like us, were born ignorant of a higher reality. And as that ignorance passed from generation to generation, an entire civilization developed based on the presumption that nothing exists "outside" of human reality because there's no evidence for such "things." With only that presumption to rely on, humanity now finds itself stranded in a highly variable reality given to errors, disputes, and conflicts and lacking in stable, eternal qualities.

In response to that situation, humanity's major "project" has been to attempt to bring order and uniformity to that chaos through social reforms, technology, and what's generally called "progress." Indeed, multiple pursuits have contributed to the overall project, and the struggles to carry out those pursuits, as well as the struggles between them, have generated the ever increasing complexity of our current civilization.

Each of the major pursuits has its own way of introducing uniformity and universality into what would otherwise be a reality of chaos and uncertainty:

1) *Religion:* "An eternal, stable reality of universal qualities ("God") exists and gives rise to ("creates") human reality."

2) *Philosophy:* "An eternal, stable reality of universal qualities ("the thing in itself") exists and gives rise to ("causes" or "conditions") human reality."

3) *Science:* "An eternal, stable reality of universal qualities ("scientific laws") exists and gives rise to human reality."

4) *The arts*: "An eternal, stable reality of universal beauty ("aesthetics") exists and informs the proper way of living in human reality."

5) *Politics:* "An eternal, stable reality of universal values ("ethics") exists and informs the proper way of living in human reality."

Unfortunately, none of the five pursuits has ever managed to transcend its own limitations, leaving it bounded by the logical absurdity of its own position. I will explain below.

The first two pursuits put themselves in the problematic position of stating the existence of an eternal reality ("God" or "thing in itself") and then either not supporting the assertion at all by relying on faith or supporting the assertion by using an argument that relies on a contradictory definition of eternal reality ("something eternal, absolute, and universal that is nonetheless detectable in human history").

The third pursuit attempts to avoid the problems of the first two by deducing the existence of an eternal reality from evidence rather than merely asserting its existence. However, this approach is just as logically contradictory as the first two because it attempts to detect evidence of something eternal and unchanging ("scientific laws") within the transitory, impermanent world of human history.

Finally, the last two pursuits, the arts and politics, much like religion, find themselves in the problematic position of asserting the existence of eternal values and then failing to support that assertion beyond referencing an authority in the government or the arts who is upheld as the embodiment of those values. The logical problems with that attitude are obvious.

Thus, we see that a logical incoherence underlies all of civilization's "progressive" pursuits owing to the fact each of them attempts to identify something (or evidence of something) eternal, absolute and unchanging in a world that can only be ever-changing, relative and prone to error.

The fact that humanity has nonetheless pursued those activities for many centuries despite their incoherence is, I believe, a testament to our lower herd instincts rather than to any real pursuit of transcendence. Indeed, those five pursuits are ultimately supported only by the persuasion and charisma of authority figures rather than by the logic and rationality we hold so dear when we proclaim ourselves intelligent, thoughtful creatures.

Now, it's a basic belief of this author that the current state of affairs -- the disputes, restlessness, and drama -- could be avoided if each of us first *learned* (or *recognized*) that certainty and eternal stability do exist but only *outside* human reality. If such a *recognition* formed the basis on which we lived, we might no longer feel the need to pursue logically incoherent activities like philosophy and science. Instead, we would detach from human reality and simply recognize it for what it is: a lower material reality governed by a higher nonmaterial reality.

This author believes we as a civilization need nihilism now to help us collectively experience the recognition I described in the previous paragraph. Having experienced that recognition, we are then free to develop a new set of human pursuits founded on a logically secure foundation that incorporates parts of both the lower and the higher realities. Because those would be totally new kinds of human pursuits, they would have no name just yet – but they will soon, and with this book, the author is making a lead contribution to their founding and establishment.

For God's sake, let us sit upon the ground,
And tell sad stories of the death of kings!

- Richard II

II.
Beyond Words & Machines: Transcending Democracy, Capitalism, and Technology

Contents

Author's Introduction: Rebellion & Reform

The 12,000-word essay you hold in your hands serves as a companion piece and a long-form introduction to my prior book *Aiming Higher Than Mere Civilization*, which I wrote in the mid-2000s but published only recently in 2014. While both volumes are written in an unadorned prose style emphasizing clarity and logical rigor, they differ significantly in their purpose.

Aiming Higher is a kind of instruction manual, with a step-by-step explanation of the philosophy of skeptical nihilism and how to practice it in one's daily life. In contrast, *Beyond Words & Machines* is a piece of polemical prose, making the case, not too stridently I hope, for the overturning of our current civilization through the widespread practice of skeptical nihilism.

As the reader knows if he or she has read *Aiming Higher*, skeptical nihilism is designed to help people discard their acquired beliefs and knowledge about the world in order to make way for a new set of beliefs they choose intentionally and rationally based on their vision of a specified future life. That is to say, the purpose of skeptical nihilism is to free people entirely from their past, to place them securely in the present, and finally to allow them to envision their future in clear and no uncertain terms.

The subtitle of *Beyond Words & Machines – Transcending Democracy, Capitalism, and Technology* – is chosen carefully, if also with an eye toward provocation. Nonetheless, I must make some clarifying remarks regarding it.

Throughout *Aiming Higher*, I write of 'transcending' or 'leaving behind' civilization. Based on critical but positive responses from readers of that book, I've concluded that the word 'civilization,' in today's American parlance anyway, is understood primarily in contrast to terms like 'primitivism'. Thus, several thoughtful readers concluded that *Aiming Higher* is arguing for a 'back-to-nature' philosophy or a Luddite-type ideology. While the book's method is compatible with either of those approaches, it was not my intention to favor or promote them.

Indeed, on my view, 'transcending' civilization or any other social organization simply involves emotionally detaching from it, becoming indifferent to it, *even while continuing to function within its protocols*. In other words, transcending civilization, as I understand the process, leads to a significant calming or cooling of one's emotional and intellectual attitude toward civil society, not to literally leaving behind all social intercourse and running off to the hills or a Himalayan cave.

That is a very important point, first of all because simply running off to the hills does not ensure you have transcended civilization if you find yourself constantly thinking about it either positively or negatively, and second of all because the whole point of skeptical nihilism is to trigger a change in an *internal state*, a change in *perspective*, not a change in external state like relocating to a new residence.

Thus, the phrase 'transcending democracy, capitalism, and technology' refers to becoming intellectually and emotionally detached from those systems – i.e., turning one's interests and passions away from them – all in preparation for the founding of a new kind of civil society guided by a new set of philosophical principles.

Lastly, I want to conclude this introduction by emphasizing that the act of transcendence, as I describe it above, is one of the most rebellious and adversarial acts possible to undertake in the context of present-day Western civilization. That's because the central features of transcendence – detachment, equanimity, absence of drama, letting go – are the very antithesis of the social habits celebrated by democracy and free-market capitalism, habits like passion, busyness, dramatic discussion, and immediate satisfaction of desire.

Thus, when you commit to skeptical nihilism, you are necessarily becoming an adversary and a harsh critic of civilization. Moreover, to the extent you succeed in transcending civilization, you may decide to encourage others to do the same, exactly as I'm doing here. In that case, you're not only an adversary of civilization but also a reformer of it. If history serves as a guide, we might conclude that adversaries and reformers, much like religious prophets, don't have the easiest time of it, so it's critical that anyone undertaking these exercises has a strong sense of courage and commitment. Indeed, if there is any optimism to be had here – and I genuinely believe there is (more on that below) – it can only come at the cost of playing the role of the adversary, playing the role, that is, of Satan.

Both *Aiming Higher* and *Beyond Words & Machines* are inspired by a series of events that occurred in my personal life in the late 1990s. Taken together, the two books offer a radically new approach to thinking, feeling, and living daily life. They also serve as a blueprint for new ways of ordering our societies and communities, educating our children, managing our economies, and organizing our politics. In short, the two books offer a blueprint for a new kind of society. Whether it's a 'better' society than what we have now is something each reader must decide for himself or herself. Obviously I believe it is better, much better, otherwise I would never have been inspired to publish the two books.

Introductory Dialogue

-- *"Are you familiar with the reality called 'Planet Earth'? You ever been there?"*

-- *"Yes, I'm very familiar with that reality. I have been there. In fact, once upon a time I spent a lot of time on Planet Earth, although I don't follow its history much anymore, just occasionally checking in remotely to monitor its activity."*

-- *"Well, I've heard a lot about Planet Earth, and I've been offered a chance to begin a series of visits. But before I make a decision, I'm hoping you could tell me something about the place. What's the attraction anyway?"*

-- *"First of all, a series of visits to Planet Earth can last a very long time, and once you start the series, the higher-ups here in our reality won't let you stop and depart from Planet Earth until you complete the entire series to their satisfaction."*

-- *"Yes, they already informed me of that, and I'm fine with the arrangement."*

-- *"Ha-ha, sure, you say that now, but once you're caught up in all the 'turmoil,' as I call it, you may have a different opinion."*

-- *"Yeah, okay, I understand. Anyway, tell me about how Planet Earth is different from what we got up here."*

-- *"Sure. First, I'll tell you how it's the same: exactly like our reality, the Planet Earth reality is a bipartite reality, meaning it has an external aspect and internal aspect, an outer world and an inner world, an outer world of perception – there they have five senses – and an inner world of belief, will, and imagination. Also like here, those two worlds are constantly interacting with one another."*

-- *"Okay. So what's the basic difference?"*

-- *"The basic difference is that the Planet Earth reality has apparently inverted the relationship between the external and internal worlds compared to how the two worlds interact here in our reality."*

-- *"Explain."*

-- *"So, as you know, here in our reality, the internal world – our 'imagination' or 'mind' in combination with our 'will' – causes or creates the external world. Agree?"*

-- *"Of course."*

-- *"Well, the reigning belief – call it 'The Core Belief' – in the Planet Earth reality is exactly the reverse. The occupants there believe that the external world causes the internal world, that physical matter or some aspect of it – like the laws of physics or the brain – causes the internal world of psychology, giving rise to mental activities such as the imagination and will."*

-- *"Whoa, so the fundamental laws of creation are reversed in the Planet Earth reality?"*

-- *"No, of course not, that's impossible. Please pay attention. What's different there is the belief that the fundamental laws of creation are reversed. In fact, the fundamental laws are just as intact there as they are here, and the Planet Earth reality functions exactly like ours – it has to. Nonetheless, almost no one there believes that's the case. Instead, they believe the opposite: they believe causality works from the* outside in *rather than from the* inside out.

-- "Sounds frustrating, like everything is always out of their control, like their minds completely lack influence over the external world. Sounds terrible. Why don't they just conclude that The Core Belief is wrong, discard it, then behave like we do here in our reality?"

-- "It sounds terrible to us, but to them it's common sense, so they see no reason to discard The Core Belief. In fact, the laws underlying their science assume The Core Belief is true. As a result, the physical disorder and randomness Earth occupants detect in their external reality is considered an intrinsic part of that reality, whereas, in fact, the external disorder and randomness is directly caused by the disorder and randomness of their poorly controlled minds. Collectively, the occupants of Planet Earth are projecting their own internal disorder onto the outer world, then erroneously concluding the disorder they perceive and measure exists independent of them. To suggest otherwise, as I am here, is considered foolishness and insanity by Earth occupants."

-- "Unbelievable. How can they have their minds so confidently made up and yet have things so reversed, so exactly backward relative to how all realities actually work?"

-- "To answer your question, I need to explain how the Planet Earth reality sustains itself."

-- "Please do."

-- "When individuals like yourself get an invitation to begin a series of visits there, a series of so-called 'lifetimes,' the first thing they must accept is the concept of 'birth,' because birth is the entranceway to that reality. It's the only way to get inside the Planet Earth reality and experience it fully. While it's true there are other ways to monitor Planet Earth and its goings-on from 'on high,' as it were, the only way to live it, experience it, and learn from it is to be 'born' there."

-- *"Okay."*

-- *"Now here's the rub: the process of being born in the Planet Earth reality requires that the visitor – someone like you or me – forget where they came from."*

-- *"You mean forget the very existence of this reality we occupy right now?"*

-- *"Exactly right. I mean forget all aspects of this reality, up to and including our friendship and this conversation we're having now. I mean forget the very existence of this reality. I mean forget even the abstract conception of this reality."*

-- *"Damn. I can hardly imagine that. Pun intended."*

-- *"As a result of this 'forgetful birth,' as I call it, when you enter the Planet Earth reality, you are automatically at the mercy of frantic, ongoing activity completely alien to you, activity that has little in common with the reality you just departed from, this reality."*

-- *"Then how can you function there?"*

-- *"At first, you cannot function there at all, you are helpless. So you have to learn to function over a long period of time, undergoing a process called 'growing up' or 'maturing,' which requires the involvement of a great many people over as many as twenty years, sometimes longer, sometimes shorter. Nonetheless, once you have learned what you need, once you have become an 'adult,' you are considered fully functional by your peers."*

-- *"Okay."*

-- *"Now please consider the most important implication of the entire process I just described. Because you and everyone else entering the Planet Earth reality have forgotten about even the existence of our reality here, much less your prior experience of it, most of the things you know while you exist in the Planet Earth reality are things you learn there, things you learn from all the people who help you grow up and mature. Thus, by the time you are an adult, you know only what other people have put into your head. No matter how intelligent, how creative you are, no matter how much of a so-called 'genius' you are, you can only know, at best, variations on what other people taught you – and the same applies to your teachers and parents, and to their teachers and parents, going back forever, generation upon generation."*

-- "Yes, I think I can see where you're going with this: growing up in the Planet Earth reality is like the blind leading the blind, or the ignorant leading the ignorant. Generation after generation teaches the same basic ideas, theories, and beliefs to each other, all of which may be wrong or false or at least highly limiting compared to the way our reality and other 'higher' realities function."

-- "Exactly. So, returning to the earlier part of our conversation – you asked why the occupants of the Planet Earth reality cannot realize The Core Belief is wrong and discard it. The short answer is – they don't discard it because they've convinced each other it is correct, it is right, it is The Truth. Moreover, they have built what are called 'civilizations,' that is, vast, complex social organizations, based on The Core Belief, civilizations that celebrate the consequences of holding that belief generation after generation, consequences like science, technology, democracy, and free market capitalism."

-- "Wait. 'Science, technology, democracy, and free market capitalism.' What do those words mean?"

-- "Ha-ha, you will learn soon enough. You may even be tempted to become a scientist, an engineer, a politician, an investor, an entrepreneur, or a manager when you grow up. We all go through those phases, those lifetimes – I certainly did. It's all just too tempting, the success, the fame and adulation, the wealth. There is real pleasure in the Planet Earth reality."

-- "But who the hell wants the pleasure if you learned everything you know from people who are under the spell of The Core Belief and who therefore have no idea that the actual laws are reversed in the 'higher' realities? Why would I want to learn anything only to be increasingly ignorant and deceived? Jesus, this is all getting very depressing."

-- *"As it should. But it's not the end of the story. It's only the first half of the story, you might say."*

-- *"So what's the second half?"*

-- *"The second half of the story is figuring out how to remember the higher reality you came from even while you occupy and function in the Planet Earth reality."*

-- *"Huh? I thought you just went to great lengths explaining that memory of our higher reality here is impossible, given the requirement of entering the Planet Earth reality via the forgetful birth process."*

-- *"Let's be clear: entering the Earth Reality through the birth canal is only possible by first forgetting your 'higher origins,' at least for now. However, every* adult *in the Earth Reality also has the opportunity to remember, to regain knowledge of their higher origins if – and this is a big 'if' –* if *they so choose to live a certain kind of life on Earth. Please be sure you understand that."*

-- *"Okay. I think I do understand it, but I'm still surprised by this new information given everything else you said before."*

-- *"Fair enough. Still, it's not that surprising when you consider the Earth Reality is not a totally isolated reality. It shares fundamental characteristics with all realities, especially our own reality here. In that regard, you might say Planet Earth is our 'neighbor reality.' In fact, it's impossible to seal off the Earth Reality from our reality or from any other higher reality, no matter the level of ignorance of the people residing there. Consequently, any adult occupant of Earth may – again, <u>if they so choose</u> – learn to remember the higher realities through all kinds of sources, including certain philosophical books, certain works of art, a variety of esoteric and occult practices, or simply discussions with other people who themselves have achieved a measure of memory of the higher realities, discussions like the one we're having right now. Indeed, while I resided on Planet Earth, I devised a philosophical method known as skeptical nihilism to help people remember."*

-- *"Okay. But if I understand the gist of everything else you've said to me, those feats of memory are nonetheless rare in any historical era on Earth. Right?"*

-- *"Indeed, you are right – they are rare. By my informal estimate, at any given time on Earth, perhaps 99% of the occupants who experience a series of lifetimes will experience only a long series of ignorant, forgetful lifetimes. Nonetheless, there's the remaining 1% of occupants, the ones who struggle and manage to remember where they came from while still alive. And the second half of this story must focus on them."*

-- *"Who are they?"*

-- *"Well, you're looking at one of them right before you. And I have a feeling you may turn out to be one of the 1% as well. That's why we're having this conversation at all – not because I have nothing better to do but because I recognize myself in you. I see myself as I was before I began my series of trips to the Earth Reality so many years ago. Now, listen to the rest of what I have to say very, very closely."*

-- *"Believe me, I'm all ears."*

Chapter 1 – The Goal: A New Perspective

The sustained application of skeptical nihilism to all aspect of one's life ultimately results in a new perspective, **a perspective that exists transcendent to (= independent of, outside of) humanity, outside of civilization, outside of democracy, capitalism, technology, and all other possible human endeavors**.

Can the reader imagine such a perspective?

Can the reader see the value in such a perspective?

Can the reader appreciate that the difference between one's current perspective, which originates within humanity, and the new perspective, which originates outside humanity, is **a process of transformation**?

The new perspective allows each of us to experience our world and reality in the much broader context of multiple worlds and multiple realities. It allows us to experience our own lives in the broader context of multiple lifetimes. The new perspective also reveals how those multiple lifetimes, multiple worlds, and multiple realities affect, influence, and cause one another, how they change one another, how one alteration to any one of those realities ripples through all possible realities.

For all that, the new perspective is **internal**, as all perspectives must be, **originating inside our minds and imaginations**. Consequently, the new perspective cannot be detected, recorded, or observed by machines and scientific instrumentation. Indeed, one of the first steps to discovering the new perspective is to turn away from all machines and instrumentation, to quiet all discussion, to suspend the use of our five senses, and pay attention solely to our innate, internal processes of logical thought, emotion, imagination, and memory.

The transformation to a new perspective can only occur in the above manner, as any perspective is first and foremost a *psychological* feature of our lives, a *private* attitude, an *asocial*, even an *antisocial* feeling. Therefore, the new perspective is not something we can detect in data, capture in descriptions, or depict in diagrams. The new perspective is indeed beyond words and machines.

As we move forward into this transformation process, everything hinges on our understanding of the nature of the new perspective. The better we understand its nature, the more deeply we appreciate that the process of transformation is not about discovering something external like knowledge or evidence – it's about discovering something internal. Consequently, the transformation must be a non-empirical, non-scientific event we experience personally, privately, and quietly.

The value of the new perspective lies in the fact it gives us a much wider choice of options in our daily lives compared to the perspective we are all born with. I simply assert here – each reader must discover this point for himself or herself – that the wider choice of options includes influencing inert and biological matter directly with mental processes. The wider choice of options also includes 'seeing' into possible futures and possible pasts, as well as experiencing multiple nonhuman realities even while remaining 'anchored' to a human body. In short, the new perspective gives each of us access to abilities that are considered 'science fiction' and delusional when considered from our 'old' perspective, the perspective each of us is born with.

The value of the new perspective also lies in the fact it is intrinsically unbiased and thus views all human beings with genuine compassion, existing outside humanity, outside biology, outside of time and space, unconditioned by any particular historical, social, cultural, or ethnic viewpoint.

Importantly, the unbiased nature of the new perspective suggests it is the optimal 'place' from which to develop not only a moral philosophy and a system of ethics but also a rigorous system of scientific investigation that no longer depends on instruments like microscopes and telescopes but only on our most immediate, most intimate perceptions, thoughts, and memories.

In short, the new perspective offers greater clarity of perception and significantly better personal control versus any perspective conditioned by our current civilization.

Chapter 2 – The Means: Skeptical Nihilism

The means of transforming our old, 'earth-bound' perspective into the new perspective described above is a method I developed over the past two decades called 'skeptical nihilism.' The method is a synthesis of ideas and practices I selected from three general areas of human endeavor: Western academic philosophy, Western occultism, and Eastern religions (various schools of Buddhism mostly).

The companion volume *Aiming Higher Than Mere Civilization* outlines in detail how the method works. In short, it applies the innate processes of logical reasoning to the imagination and memory, allowing us to transcend all possible human beliefs and behaviors (including skeptical nihilism itself), i.e., to rise above, to go beyond material reality and therefore beyond all words and machines. In so doing, skeptical nihilism paves the way for us to discover and 'taste' the new perspective described in Chapter 1.

Only after having accessed the new perspective and habituated ourselves to it, may we then set aside the practice of skeptical nihilism, as it will have fully served its purpose. However, until we've achieved stable access, skeptical nihilism remains our only real means of securing the new perspective. Therein lies the fundamental importance of this paradoxical method.

In this brief section, I list what I consider the defining (and somewhat technical) features of skeptical nihilism. Keeping those features in mind as you read the rest of this book will help you understand the method's inherent difficulties and challenges.

Skeptical nihilism is formal: the method is more about form than about content – i.e., the method aims for a perspective, a view, an attitude (form), not for a particular set of facts, a piece of evidence, or a theory (content).

Skeptical nihilism is oppositional: the method puts one at odds with society, converting one into a critic of humanity. The method turns on the paradox of harshly criticizing humanity even while affirming its existence. Indeed, the method may ultimately leave the practitioner feeling stranded with a teaching that is incommunicable. Unsurprisingly, those who do not practice the method may see its practitioners as antisocial and psychopathic – in a word, 'satanic' – despite the fact the practitioners also profess a deep compassion for humanity.

Skeptical nihilism is internal: the method is more about psychology than about sociology, politics, and technology. That's because the method starts from the raw, subjective experience of the individual not from external teachings and instrumental data. In other words, the method strives to abolish the influence of received education.

Skeptical nihilism is visionary: the method is more about imagination and subjective experience than about discussion, argument, and public debate.

Skeptical nihilism is timeless: the method puts one at odds with both historical traditions and technological progress, both of which are considered, at best, temporary distractions, or, at worst, fashionable lies.

Skeptical nihilism is spiritual: the method is more focused on the importance of nonmaterial reality than on material reality.

Skeptical nihilism is powerful: the method is more about directly controlling one's life experience through will and intention than about electing an external authority to control or 'manage' one's life experience. In other words, the method puts one at odds with governments and other management structures, whether founded on tyrannical principles, on one extreme, or republican principles, on the other.

Considered as a group, the above features of skeptical nihilism illustrate ***a method centered on the immediate experience of the human being*** not on experiences mediated by outside sources such as schools, governments, corporations, religions, and scientific experts.

The method is ***personal, psychological, and philosophical***, rather than social, material, and scientific. Employing the method requires only one's immediate perceptions of the world and one's mental processes, including emotion, memory, and imagination. At no point does the method involve a laboratory apparatus, a machine, a gadget, any piece of technology.

To practice skeptical nihilism properly, every practitioner must learn to respect, value, and trust his or her individual, immediate experience of life over the 'authority' of the outside world, whether that authority be the fashions of a crowd, the experience of a trained expert, or the data and theories of a research scientist.

Chapter 3 – Skeptical Nihilism's Predecessors: Idealism, Criticism, and Pessimism

To better understand what skeptical nihilism is and is not, it's helpful to consider some of the philosophical trends that feed into it. Rather than embark on a history of ideas (which I do in the subsequent essay *Skeptical*

Nihilism and the Feast of Creation), here I briefly address a few key intellectual sources.

Skeptical nihilism inherits from **idealism** the basic view that nonmaterial (so-called 'mental') forces give rise to and shape material reality in some manner.

Skeptical nihilism inherits from all forms of **criticism** the basic view that observation, evaluation, comparison, and judgment are necessary prerequisites to the clear understanding of anything.

Skeptical nihilism inherits from **pessimism** the basic view that cultural progress is an illusion, in some fundamental sense, and that humanity, *only when considered in isolation or as an end in itself*, has no intrinsic meaning or value.

Unsurprisingly, then, skeptical nihilism serves as a tool for transcending the materialistic, humanistic, progressive activities of human reality and society, including democratic politics, capitalist economics, technology, and empirical science.

Also unsurprisingly, the participants of a civilization engrossed in those materialistic activities (as ours clearly is) may have great difficulty finding value in skeptical nihilism. They will likely see only destructive impulses in the method, impulses to 'tear down' or 'discard' cherished beliefs which, over the centuries, have given rise to the civilized world now surrounding us. Indeed, relative to the so-called 'achievements' of our current civilization, effective application of skeptical nihilism by a great many people would seem to leave us with nothing but decay and rubble.

However, the error or, let us say, the 'limitation' of the above interpretation of skeptical nihilism lies in its failure to *imagine* an alternative society in place of the rubble. Having become so caught up in, so entranced by beliefs in 'progress' and 'technological advancement,' the above interpretation falsely assumes those beliefs must reflect the best possible future. Thus, if those beliefs fail to hold in the face of skeptical nihilism, the only reasonable conclusion *seems* to be that some form of catastrophe or apocalypse must follow. In short, the interpretation suffers from a fundamental failure of the imagination, failing to envision how our present-day economic, political, and scientific institutions (which, by the way, everyone admits are imperfect and, in many ways, frustrating to individual growth) might be replaceable by something better.

In contrast to the above view and much like its philosophical predecessors, the method of skeptical nihilism encourages us to use our imaginations to more clearly envision the difference between where we are now and where we could be, and to do so with sufficient courage to understand that on the other side of the destruction of our current civilization is something immeasurably, indeed, *inconceivably* superior to what we have now, something far more magnificent than mere rubble and ruins.

Chapter 4 – Sustaining the New Perspective: Imagination

The faculty of imagination is so important to skeptical nihilism that it deserves a section of its own. But before we discuss its importance to our method, let's briefly consider the total inadequacy of Western approaches to understanding imagination. Indeed, it's no wonder there's such a widespread, collective fear of the power of human imagination in our current society, given that our accepted scientific theories barely account for its existence much less attempt to explain its function.

Physical sciences like physics, chemistry, and molecular biology don't consider themselves obligated to address the existence of imagination in their theories, despite the fact the use of the faculty is wholly responsible for those sciences existing in the first place. Meanwhile, social sciences like psychology, though obviously acknowledging the existence of imagination, do little more to account for its function than to use a crude, descriptive methodology. Finally, philosophers have been entangled in a fruitless, centuries-long attempt to 'reduce' imagination (and other purely subjective experience) to material substrates like the brain.

The upshot of the above situation is that imagination (indeed, subjective experience as a whole) has been rather 'swept under the rug' in academic research, either ignored, as in disciplines like chemistry, or treated like a strange anomaly, as in much of cognitive science and the philosophy of mind. Making matters worse, it seems that at this juncture in history it's asking far too much of scientists that they admit they got it all wrong from the beginning: they developed theories that adequately predict the behavior of celestial bodies and subatomic particles while failing to predict or control the behavior of their own minds.

Indeed, pointing out the obvious to physicists, chemists, and biologists – namely, that their theories fail to address seriously the central role imagination plays in our lives – results in looks of incomprehension on their part, as if to say, "Sorry, but that's not our responsibility – we don't 'do' subjective experience. If it's not something we can measure quantitatively, it has no place in our theories of the universe. Consequently, we are under no obligation to modify the foundations of our theories to account for the existence and function of human imagination."

Thus, rather than suffer through the equivalent of a nervous breakdown and then pick up the pieces to construct a truly comprehensive theory of human reality, a theory uniting objective and subjective experience at its very foundation, scientists have chosen the more 'expedient' solution of going into denial, conveniently but erroneously treating the phenomenon of imagination as if it didn't deserve the same treatment as biological tissues, rocks, and stars, as if it were a kind of internal vapor hardly deserving of any rigorous theory at all.

A knock-on effect of those scientific misunderstandings has been the wholesale devaluation of imagination in everyday life. Indeed, despite being one of the most intimate of human experiences, imagination is inevitably treated as a kind of side-show to 'real life,' becoming little more than a receptacle for idle daydreaming, the basic equivalent of an internal television channel useful for passing time when a real TV isn't convenient. Still worse, many people from a very early age become frightened or ashamed of their own imagination, unwilling to give the faculty full rein for fear of what they might find there. Perhaps the only social group who has found value in imagination is creative artists who, unfortunately, have little influence in a highly materialistic society like our own.

In contrast to what I describe above, imagination plays a central role in the method and practice of skeptical nihilism.

Firstly, the proper application of skeptical nihilism requires extensive use of the imagination to envision clearly all the scenarios implied by various belief systems. To achieve the goal of transcending all possible systems of belief, one must at least be able to envision the concrete implications of those beliefs and, in some sense, role-play the scenarios they potentially give rise to. The only consistent way of doing that is through rigorous application of one's imagination.

Secondly, having successfully completed the exercise of skeptical nihilism, transcending all possible belief systems, and reestablishing one's identity in the nonmaterial, transcendental realms, one must continue to rely on the imagination to envision one's future life and goals and to project them, as it were, from internal reality into external reality. Thus, imagination serves as the engine and driver of creation in the material world.

Clearly, in skeptical nihilism the faculty of imagination represents something far deeper than a receptacle for daydreaming or a tool for imagining the contents of a novel. It represents the most immediate link we have *in daily life* to a higher reality, and in that sense it is just as valuable, if not more valuable, than our daily experience of the 'tangible' world of matter.

Chapter 5 – When All Is 'Said' And Done: Triumph

One's experience of the entire transformation process from beginning to end – taking up the method of skeptical nihilism, seeing the practice through to its completion, afterwards stabilizing oneself in the new perspective beyond every possible form of human society and civilization – yes, one's ultimate experience is that of ***triumph***, triumph over oneself, triumph over civilization's charming beliefs and efficient systems, triumph over democracy, capitalism, technology, empirical science, and religion.

For all that, the sense of triumph results from winning a painful, protracted war most certainly, a war waged against oneself, not against other people. Indeed, it's about becoming victorious *against* oneself, if we can allow ourselves to imagine such a thing. And if we cannot yet imagine it, well, I don't feel sorry for any of us because we are all in the same boat *at first*. That is to say, we are all born equal: equally stupid, equally ignorant of the higher realities, equally possessed by the obsessions of civilization – and therefore equally at odds with our true selves.

The open question is this: how many of us can successfully complete the process I describe here and in *Aiming Higher*? And having experienced the triumph, how can we help other people experience it? How can we use the momentum of our *personal transformation* to help accelerate a *societal transformation* that finally drives a *political transformation*? *How can we convert a growing number of private triumphs into a unified, long-term public triumph?* – that is the open question.

This book envisions a future where it becomes fashionable to turn away from the deceptions and distractions of a broken civilization to focus, first, on ourselves individually and, second, on society as a whole – a future when philosophical and psychological activity takes precedence over engineering and technological activity, when simply sitting in a chair in a quiet room everyday, perhaps several hours everyday, takes precedence over staring at screens, driving cars, and talking – a future where we strive to transcend, to rise above words and machines.

Perhaps during that period of societal and political transformation – and it won't last forever, so perhaps consider it a 'tech sabbatical' – our technological progress will languish for a time, and we will value it less, but that situation won't concern us because we'll also know that the computers, televisions, mobile devices, aircraft, and power grids will still be there when we return from our interior work, ready for us to use them in a much 'wiser' fashion than before.

Chapter 6 – Special Topics

a) Smashing the Infamies of Science and Technology

The roots of the next societal transformation exist where today's science fails, and today's science fails exactly where it fails to acknowledge its own inbuilt limitations. Right at that point – where the imperceptible and the inconceivable 'begin' to exist – today's science reveals its major limitation by denying the value, indeed the very existence, of the imperceptible and the inconceivable. And to the extent each of us works, lives, and understands our lives within the accepted scientific framework, each of us shares in that limitation: we also fail to value the imperceptible and the inconceivable. We may also deny those 'things' exist, embracing some form of atheism, becoming full-blown empiricists, sensualists, and materialists in the process.

Our collective failure to recognize the inbuilt limitations of science and technology derives most immediately from our failure to use our innate powers of skeptical inquiry. Whereas once upon a time we relied on those powers to smash the idols of religion and monarchy, for the last two centuries we have put those powers 'on hold' when evaluating the idols of science and technology.

Our failure to use skeptical reasoning to evaluate science has led not only to the idolization of science but, more insidiously, to the enthronement of science as a form of common sense. We even describe our current state of affairs as 'progress' or 'scientific advancement,' as if our tools, machines, and gadgets have made us smarter, more knowledgeable, more perceptive than our superstitious forefathers – in a phrase, *as if our civilization were better than rather than merely different from civilizations of the past.*

Today we find ourselves seemingly incapable of standing outside science and skeptically evaluating it. Instead, we worship it.

The purpose of *Beyond Words & Machines* and *Aiming Higher Than Mere Civilization* is to remind us all again how to put skeptical inquiry front and center in our lives, how to use its methods not only to smash the idol of empirical science but also to build the foundations of a new approach to living, an approach founded first and foremost on a transcendental, non-empirical reality, a reality imperceptible and inconceivable, i.e., a reality that exists beyond words and machines.

Naturally, my message is reformist, revolutionary, radical, and, given the current state of affairs, highly idealistic. For all that, it may at least offer a guidepost to a new social and cultural order, an order where our materialist world continues to exist but only within the larger context of a nonmaterial world, a world beyond the limits of science and religion.

The purpose of applying the method of skeptical nihilism to science, engineering, and technology is not to prove that those pursuits are, in some sense, false – rather, it's to demonstrate the intrinsic limitations of those pursuits and to discourage us from the fruitless task of trying to find real advancement using them.

In centuries past, the predecessors of skeptical nihilism (various forms of critique and idealism) successfully demonstrated the limits of authoritarian religious and political structures, leading to the grand achievements of the American and French Revolutions. Unfortunately, having been freed from the 'hypnosis' of kings and popes, civilization has turned to other idols since 1800, first empirical science, then free-market capitalism, finally empty-headed democracy.

While we may consider ourselves wise enough never again to worship human beings appointed to royal and religious leadership roles, we nonetheless fall into a collective trance at the mention of nonhuman idols like 'scientific evidence,' 'market efficiency,' and 'majority rule,' failing to grasp the limitations intrinsic to those ideas because we fail step outside of them – ***thus the need for a method like skeptical nihilism whose fundamental purpose is to help us transcend the very things we cherish out of fear and ignorance***.

Indeed, skeptical nihilism is straightforward and transparent, assuming only the minimal and most obvious to demonstrate how so much that we consider 'true' or 'right' is no more true or right than what we consider 'false' or 'wrong.' The method's goal is *never* to declare any particular idea, theory, or belief true (including, paradoxically, skeptical nihilism itself), rather to demonstrate that all ideas, theories, and beliefs are unavoidably 'stuck' in a certain time and place, are therefore at best relatively true and thus logically incapable of transcending their own time and reaching universal validity.

In other words, the method cuts off the 'urge to the Absolute' within the world of our senses, forcing us to find the Absolute, if it does exist, outside of our senses in a realm transcendental to or 'above' our everyday, common-sense world. Having cut-off the urge to the Absolute in this world, skeptical nihilism forces our awareness into a higher state of being, where 'we' *must* adopt the new perspective described above in Chapter 1, a perspective 'beyond' all human pursuits.

Established in that perspective, 'we' have effectively smashed the infamies of science and technology (among other infamies). Indeed, we are no longer at the mercy of any theory or idea, including skeptical nihilism itself. 'We' may pick and choose theories as 'we' see fit based on any criteria 'we' see fit. Thus, 'we' are no longer compelled to take sides and fight for this or that scientific, economic, social, or political idea. From our new perspective, all ideas, all worldviews exist on the same plane, as it were, and none is any more superior to any other except relative to criteria 'we' arbitrarily choose.

By not taking sides, the new perspective is intrinsically compassionate, never labelling human activities 'good' and 'evil' or 'true' and 'false' unless the goal is to play the 'game' of dualistic morality. As such, the activity of life remains a game, a *ludibrium* – i.e., a self-contained pursuit, perhaps played according to set rules, with accepted limitations, never to be taken too seriously, perhaps even mocked and ridiculed.

To put the last few paragraphs in the context of our current state of affairs, and to help the reader better appreciate how distant we are from seeing the method of skeptical nihilism work its 'magic' on society, let's consider how we might expect a scientist to react to reading this book and its companion *Aiming Higher Than Mere Civilization*.

First of all, because most practicing scientists don't believe empirical science has intrinsic conceptual limitations, we can expect them to reject the fundamental premise of skeptical nihilism, as they would see no need for anything like a societal transformation that leads to the abandonment of science.

While scientists certainly acknowledge that no single scientific field or theory can ever claim to have arrived at the proper theory that applies to the universe forever, they nonetheless also claim that science, being iterative by nature, may eventually arrive at such a theory and perhaps has been approaching one as instrumentation improves. The only thing holding scientists back, the story goes, is their current state of instrumentation and their theoretical intelligence, which both continue to improve over time, a process called 'progress' or 'advancement.'

Yet the fact remains that ***science has allowed itself optimistically and self-deceptively to rely on instrumentation to determine what does and does not exist***. In other words, 'detectability by instrumentation' has become the *sine qua non* of existence. In those cases where something *by definition* is imperceptible – e.g., 'consciousness,' 'imagination' – or is inconceivable – e.g., 'God' – science either outright denies its existence, as in the latter case, or reduces that 'thing' to an arbitrary material construct to make it detectable by instrumentation, as in the former case.

In either case, given what I've stated above, the wiser approach would be for science simply to acknowledge it cannot *ever* detect the existence of 'things' like consciousness and God, and therefore it must refrain from studying and commenting upon them at all.

To put the matter in harsh (perhaps inflammatory) terms, self-deception may be the single psychological defect underlying all scientific training in much the same way it underlies most all religious belief. Without such self-deception, the innate process of skeptical nihilism would be free to remain active and critical of all belief systems, scientific or religious, effortlessly accessing the world beyond words and machines.

Seen from the context of the current practices of science and religion, the immediate goal of skeptical nihilism is thus to remove self-deception and allow free rein to our skeptical sensibilities. Having achieved that goal (no mean feat), 'we' may then perhaps achieve the secondary goal of founding a new science encompassing both the empirical (conceivable and perceptible) and the non-empirical (the inconceivable and imperceptible).

Thus, our goal here is *never* to resolve any issues within the current framework of empirical science but to begin our investigations anew, from the ground up, so to speak, building an entirely new framework that encompasses the old one. The imperceptible and inconceivable may then serve as the ground, the foundation on which a logically secure form of scientific investigation is built.

b) A Religious Interpretation of Skeptical Nihilism & the New Perspective

In this section of *Beyond Words & Machines*, perhaps the strangest section of the essay (indeed, every essay should have a 'strange section'), I intend to engage briefly in a bit of mythmaking. I would like to consider the method of skeptical nihilism in the context of 'God,' that dreaded three-letter word so cherished by religion, so reviled by empirical science, so unnecessary, in fact, to anyone involved in serious philosophical dispute.

I do this exercise mainly because there are a great many readers out there who 'believe in God,' just as there are a great many who 'have no belief in God.' Their reasons for a belief or a lack thereof do not concern me. Rather, I care about the fact that most people have some conception of 'God,' and therefore are entranced by the word, often without realizing it. So be it, let's consider how skeptical nihilism functions in worlds, universes, and realities governed by 'God.'

By the way, if the word 'God' does not interest you, you may skip this section entirely and will have missed nothing essential.

First off, to make sense of this myth, we must define the word 'God.' So be it. Here, 'God' does *not* mean a specific being, anthropomorphically or otherwise described, or a locus of spiritual power. Instead, the word 'God' means exactly and only this: 'the reality that exists independent of all possible human activity.' The first important implication of this definition is that God is 'imperceptible and inconceivable.' The second important implication of this definition is that God exists independent of reason, logic, and scientific investigation, independent of words and machines, all of which represent purely human activities.

Having thus defined 'God' and drawn out some implications of the definition, it makes sense to ask, "What is the relationship between God and humanity?"

Answering that question requires us to address the relationship between a timeless God and a temporal humanity. We must determine how those two realities interact with and influence each other. And in the process of making that determination, we will learn about the 'forgetful' birth process of every human being and the religious concept of the 'The Fall.'

Finally, we can state the myth as something like this: originating in the higher realities, 'we' are all by definition a 'part' of God. However, the energy (will, karma) inherent to any part of God may choose to turn against the rest of God, leaving behind or abandoning the other 'portion.' This process of God turning away from Himself or deflecting Himself (the higher volte-face) *creates* a new reality, a lower reality, the reality of humanity. Thus, the very existence of humanity becomes possible only subsequent to a rebellion of God against Himself.

The existence of humanity thus requires three basic spiritual or metaphysical prerequisites: a God, a rebellion of God against Himself, and a subsequent forgetting of that rebellion by humanity.

Consequently, as human beings, we cannot rebel against God. We are all, in a metaphysical sense, 'too late,' 'too low,' 'too forgetful' for that kind of rebellion. Nonetheless, as human beings, we can rebel against ourselves, against our own humanity. The process of humanity turning away from itself (the lower volte-face) returns us to the higher reality of God. That is to say, to rebel against our own humanity is to return us to God – *and that is where skeptical nihilism enters the picture*.

The purpose of skeptical nihilism is to help us successfully turn against our own (ignorant) human nature and escape the civilization we have inadvertently caged ourselves in. Having done that, we are reunited with God in some mysterious sense. End of myth.

c) The Author's Route to the New Perspective

Today, at the ripe old age of 47, I can survey my life and see what I *believe* are the broadest contours of the terrain I've traveled thus far. In total, my life may be divided into three sequential phases, each building on the prior phase(s). I *believe* those phases comprise my life's 'calling' – i.e., the reason I was born and continue to live.

Those phases are:
- Asking the right questions about life (ages 18 to 30),

- Seeking out answers to those questions (ages 30 to 42),
- Communicating those answers to the wider world (ages 42 to present).

This particular book fits into the third phase, as do the other books, fiction and nonfiction, I've published since turning 42 in the year 2009.

Considering the phases as a whole, I *believe* they illustrate a sustained, long-term 'quest for the truth,' a grandiose, nontechnical phrase that nonetheless should ring familiar to most people's ears.

I began this quest foolishly enough, guided by an insatiable desire for knowledge, learning, and experience. Initially, my quest fit into the common patterns of the culture of our day – e.g., university education, jobs in academia and at private-sector companies. However, in my thirties, the quest became significantly more esoteric and 'impractical,' not given to comprehension by many people, not capable of generating stable income or job security.

This latter turn of events was not something I had prepared for. As a result, I was thrown back on myself, as it were, with minimal material resources to survive on and any form of prosperity seemingly forever out of my grasp. Despite my deep education, my powerful critical intelligence, my generally serious and upright attitude toward daily life, I found myself increasingly at odds with the goals and pursuits of 'successful' American society. Indeed, even if only in my own mind, I had become a radical and a rebel in a society that found no value in the ideas I valued the most. Yet, at the same time, I believed and continue to believe, those ideas would benefit society tremendously – though only if it first abandoned many of the beliefs and perspectives it collectively holds so dearly today.

Meanwhile, I've been able to write and publish books and essays that attempt, in various ways, to communicate the 'wiser' perspective I've acquired, occasionally in ways that are shocking and disturbing, intentionally so. Some of those books are works of esoteric fiction masquerading as nonfiction (e.g., *Great & Mighty Things*), others are works of nonfiction inspired by actual events in my own life (e.g., *Beyond Words & Machines* and *Aiming Higher Than Mere Civilization*).

All of those books are united by a common purpose: to persuade people to embark on a 'pursuit of truth' rather than a 'pursuit of happiness.' While there is nothing intrinsic to truth that requires it to oppose happiness (as far as I can tell), the two are necessarily opposed in our current civilization. It is the purpose of *Beyond Words and Machines* to explain and illustrate the nature of that opposition and why it exists. It is the purpose of the companion volume – *Aiming Higher Than Mere Civilization* – to explain the nature of the pursuit of truth itself.

Concluding Dialogue

-- *"Well, that's some incredible information, and I'm thankful for it. Nonetheless, it's still depressing to think I will forget all of it when I'm born into the Planet Earth reality."*

-- *"Yes, but even though you must forget it, there's no reason why you cannot recover the information while residing on Planet Earth. It's just a question of the* *<u>certain kind of life</u>* *you choose to live. Those who make the 'right' life choice make it increasingly likely they will remember the higher realities where we all originate. Indeed, if you apply yourself to the task of remembering, perhaps guided by the method of skeptical nihilism, the task itself becomes the central pursuit of your adulthood, far more important than any other aspect of your personal and professional life. Those human beings who consistently pursue truth over happiness, striving to remember their origins in the higher realities rather than surrendering to idle pleasure, are members of what I called the 1% in the introductory dialogue."*

-- *"Can you please describe this 'certain kind of life,' even if only in general terms?"*

-- *"Sure. The kind of life I'm referring to can be summarized in three words:* *<u>detachment, discipline, and sacrifice</u>*. *All three of those words are perhaps summarized in the word* *<u>skeptic</u>*. *That is to say, you have a real chance of remembering where you came from, your metaphysical origins, only when you become highly skeptical, highly critical of humanity as a whole, of all its so-called achievements and advancements, of the whole human impulse to build civilizations based on efficient satisfaction of desire. There* *must also be a strong sense of loathing and disgust accompanying your skepticism."*

-- *"Okay, and now give me an example of the 'wrong' kind of life, if you could."*

-- *"Well, there's never any shortage of those examples, as they comprise the other 99% of humanity. Their kind of life can be summarized in the three words: passion, agitation, and greed. And all three of those words perhaps can be summarized by the single word believer. To put the comparison in overly stark terms, the 1% are pessimists regarding the fate of humanity, while the 99% are short-sighted optimists."*

-- *"So what's preventing more of the 99% from coming round to the 'new perspective' of the 1%?"*

-- *"Well, the last thing human beings want to do is question the intrinsic value of humanity and civilization, simply because they cannot imagine anything else beyond or independent of humanity. Therefore, criticizing humanity, expressing genuine disgust for it, even outright misanthropy, summons every human being's deepest fears of nothingness, of nonexistence. Criticism ought to summon the joy of growth into a higher form of being – that's indeed what happens in the case of the 1% - but instead, for the 99%, criticism summons fear and confusion. For that reason alone – the fear of nonexistence – serious discussion of leaving humanity behind, of abandoning all forms of biology and geology, of transferring the human impulse into a nonhuman realm, like the realm we occupy right here and now – all of those discussions almost never happen."*

-- *"Okay, okay. But what does all this have to do with the kind of life I should choose to live if I want to be in the 1%, not the 99%?"*

-- *"It has everything to do with your choice. I just told you that anyone in the 1% must, first and foremost, have a deep-set critical attitude toward all aspects of humanity, civilization, technological progress. Then I also told you how rare that attitude is, how inconceivable it is to the minds of 99% of the population. Now when you add those two points together you arrive at the following conclusion: <u>the choice of the right life must trigger</u>*

<u>the choice of a life that is at odds with 99% of the population</u>, a life that is solitary, the life of the outsider, the loner, the stranger living on the margins. Please understand this deeply. Please meditate on it."

-- *"Okay, I will. Anyway, I think I already appreciate it."*

-- *"Sure, you think you do, and I'm sure you genuinely have some real understanding of it. Nonetheless, I doubt you can fully imagine right now how difficult things will be once you are born into the Planet Earth reality and begin living there. You will likely find that making the choice of the right life is exceedingly difficult because you are constantly at odds with the pleasure-seeking crowd or herd behavior that dominates civilization. Indeed, your attitude will put you at odds with educational institutions, government institutions, businesses and corporations, often even families. Living your life on such terms, so 'against the grain' of society, can have a negative impact on you as you get older. Your life may become increasingly unpleasant even though you become increasingly wise."*

-- *"Seems like a terrible injustice built into this whole experience."*

-- *"Maybe. But we all know it doesn't have to be that way. There's every reason to believe that life on Planet Earth could become increasingly pleasant and enjoyable as you and everyone else become increasingly wise. But at least in the short term it never plays out that way."*

-- *"Why?"*

-- *"Well, because the majority of people find no short-term pleasure and satisfaction in achieving the detachment, discipline, and sacrifice necessary to become wiser."*

-- *"So let's talk about those three requirements in more detail. What kind of sacrifices are we talking about here?"*

-- *"Precisely the kinds of sacrifices described in this book and in* Aiming Higher Than Mere Civilization*."*

-- *"You mean to say the methods and exercises of skeptical nihilism are the necessary sacrifices?"*

-- *"More or less, yes. Certainly from the point of view of an ignorant society founded on the immediate satisfaction of desire and the constant drive for pleasure, those exercises – activities like sitting still in a room for long periods of time sorting through your belief systems – are tremendous sacrifices. Do you understand that?"*

-- *"Yes, I think so."*

-- *"Good – because it's a critical point. I'm not trying to frighten you or anyone else who may undertake the life of the 1%, but I am trying to be honest with you and very clear: this life I'm talking about, this path, this 'right' form of growth is distinctly at odds with what is now called 'civilization' in the Planet Earth reality. There's no getting around that fact, at least for now."*

-- *"Okay."*

-- *"Everything about the method of skeptical nihilism is at odds with civilization, at odds with progress and advancement as civilization defines those concepts. Consequently, anyone who successfully practices the method over a long period of time, indeed over the course of their entire adult life, must also find themselves at odds with civilization. That doesn't mean you have to literally leave civilization and rusticate, going off to live in a forest or a cave – though it could mean that if you want it to – but it does mean that, at the very least, you must experience a civilization that you know, you recognize is in fact a highly limited life-form not at all deserving of your higher respect."*

-- *"So someone practicing your methods is a sort of revolutionary or radical figure, right?"*

-- *"Yes, in a way the 1% are a small sect of revolutionary types – and we all know from human history how governments treat those kinds of people, with suspicion at best, violence at worst."*

-- *"Though, in fact, nowadays governments seem to have replaced the word 'revolutionary' with the word 'terrorism.' Agree?"*

-- "Please, let's not go there. But as long as you brought up the topic of terrorism, let me clarify something, an issue that always comes up when I discuss the methods of skeptical nihilism. These methods are designed to act on the mind or, more precisely if a bit redundantly, on ideas in the mind. In other words, skeptical nihilism is akin to what was once called 'idealism' among philosophers."

-- "Okay. I can see that."

-- "And because it is an idealist perspective and an idealist method, it intentionally has nothing to do with physically manipulating things in external reality."

-- "That's putting it very abstractly."

-- "Fair enough. Putting it more concretely: skeptical nihilism has nothing to do with any form of murder and destruction of property. This should come as no surprise to you, given that you and I know it's the inner world that causes the existence of the outer world, not vice versa. But 99% of human beings who have things reversed, believing the outer causes the inner, inevitably interpret skeptical nihilism as a drive to destroy civilization, to literally reduce it to rubble."

-- "Well, can you blame them for concluding that? I mean, your disgust for civilization shines through in everything you've said to me so far today."

-- "And so it does. But that disgust expresses itself as a detachment from civilization, as an indifference to it, though never does it waste time trying to destroy property and kill people. That sort of behavior simply makes no sense from my perspective."

-- "Okay."

-- "Anyway, I just wanted to be clear that skeptical nihilism has nothing in common with acts of terrorism and acts of war. If indeed the method of skeptical nihilism reduces civilization to rubble – and I frankly hope it does – it will not be because my colleagues and I resorted to physical violence but because our philosophical method and perspective irrevocably altered people's ideas about what is possible in the Planet Earth reality, causing

increasing numbers of the 99% to turn their attention away from civilization and follow other pursuits they deem more valuable than civilization. If that were to happen, I have every reason to believe civilization would decline quite rapidly without a single war or bomb detonated. That's what I hope to see, that's my vision of the future: a huge crowd of independently-minded people suddenly changing their minds in unison. *That's the ultimate paradox. With people's minds thus changed, alterations in their behavior must soon follow, the collapse of civilization then coming naturally if painfully."*

-- *"Okay. So, to bring our little discussion to a solid conclusion, could you please explain more about why making the choice of the 'right' life is so difficult and, for many, impossible."*

-- *"Yes, definitely. The difficulty can be summed up in one word:* ***distractions****, in particular, technological distractions."*

-- *"Ah, yes. The Cult of the Gadget, right?"*

-- *"Yes, the Cult of the Machine, Cult of the Gadget, Cult of the Instrument, whatever you prefer to call it. That cult has gone by many names over the past couple centuries. But of course it's not just the gadgets themselves – it's also* why *we use them, why we* believe *we need them and want them, those things, so many things and objects."*

-- *"For entertainment, for escapism."*

-- *"Sure, sometimes that's the reason. But the issue is far deeper than that. If you consider the issue further, you'll grasp that occupants of the Earth Reality use gadgets because they don't trust or believe in their innate abilities. They don't believe they even have certain abilities. For example, they don't believe they have the ability to communicate across distances with their minds; consequently, they require some kind of physical interaction. Based on that belief, they have invented gadgets like the telegraph, the telephone, and the internet. A second example – they don't believe they have the ability to heal their bodies with their minds and therefore, again, they require some kind of physical interaction. Based on that belief, they have invented literally tens of thousands of medications over the past century, the totality of which has done little to abolish disease. Indeed, quite the opposite has occurred, with clinical researchers continually discovering yet more diseases, syndromes, and conditions, all of which require still more medications to be invented. Yet everyone, experts and laymen alike, call this state of affairs 'progress' without feeling a bit doubtful or skeptical."*

-- "So it gets back to The Core Belief that limits them, holds them back."

-- "Yes. That's why I say that The Core Belief – stated negatively as 'the mind cannot directly influence the body and other physical processes' – is the ultimate distraction, for once you believe The Core Belief, once you take it for granted, consider it common sense, you are pulled so far off the path of the 'right' life that you may never find your way back. In this specific case what happens is you entirely fail to practice skeptical nihilism, fail to find any value in it, because skeptical nihilism has nothing whatsoever to do with technological gadgets and scientific instruments. Thus, at any and every turn, you confront technologies and machinery that distract, pull you away from the most sublime of all human tasks, a task that is practiced simply by sitting alone in a chair and applying one's logical reasoning to one's emotion, imagination, and memory."

-- "Or perhaps you meet someone like yourself and have a similar conversation to this in the Planet Earth reality, thus reminding yourself of the existence and value of skeptical nihilism. Right?"

-- "Ha-ha. Yes, well, one would hope for such an occurrence. But I was in that position many times during my Planet Earth visits, and let me assure you, pretty much any attempt to have this sort of conversation on Earth is doomed to failure. The reason is pretty straightforward and you probably already guessed it. <u>A conversation like the one we are having now, if both parties are to take it seriously and learn from it, must occur outside the realm of common sense</u>*. While that's easy enough for the two of us in this higher reality where Planet Earth common sense finds no purchase, down there on Earth, any attempt to dispose of common sense leads to all sorts of negative reactions from Earth occupants, including confusion, anger, derision, eye-rolling, even laughter. As a result, having this conversation we are having now in the Planet Earth reality is exceedingly rare."*

-- *"Okay. So now that I understand what the distraction is, how can I ever stand a chance of choosing the right life to avoid it?"*

-- *"You stand a chance if, from an early age, you begin developing a certain kind of personality, a certain kind of personal style, you might say. If you tend not to run with the common crowd, if you find yourself often involved in solitary activities, if you* prefer *to be alone, if you are often musing abstractly, often daydreaming, even about trivial things, often 'inside your own head,' as they say down there – if all of this describes you even as a child and adolescent, you may have a chance to find the path as an adult. And if you do find the path by, say, the age of twenty-five, you may then have a chance to apply your own version of skeptical nihilism to your own beliefs and perceptions and transcend humanity and civilization by, say, the age of thirty-five. That's my own story in broad outline. But there's no guarantee this will happen for you. "*

-- *"Well, what could go wrong?"*

-- *"What could go wrong, basically, is you finally give up. So many years of playing the role of 'outsider' starting from such an early age may start to take a toll on you emotionally and physically even in your twenties. Daily life among crowds of people so different from you and who therefore seemingly have no ability to appreciate your personal style may eventually make your life too much of a burden, leading directly to extreme measures and final conclusions."*

-- *"What?!"*

-- *"That's right. I mean to say, leading directly to insanity, suicide, or homicide, or to some kind of so-called 'freak accident' that conveniently results in your immediate death and return to this reality."*

-- *"Jesus, this conversation is sure uplifting!"*

-- *"I'm just trying to lay it all out there for you. The fact is, choosing the 'right' life and then sticking to it is a huge undertaking, made all the more difficult by the fact almost no one will understand what you are doing. How can they understand if they are all mired in what I've been calling common sense, if, unlike you, they are quite happy with their lives, with their material successes, and see no reason whatsoever to question anything deeply?"*

-- *"So, assuming I do find the right path, stick to it, successfully apply skeptical nihilism, and transcend civilization, I'm imagining myself walking around Planet Earth with the constant awareness that I am radically different from all those other people, even though I still basically look and behave like they do."*

-- *"That's right. But it's even worse than that, in a sense, because any attempt to explain yourself to them, to tell them what you've been through and how you experience life from a new perspective, will lead, at best, to confusion on their part, or, at worst, to their outright mockery of you."*

-- *"So how do you deal with it?"*

-- *"Well, as I recall, you just get used to it. In my case, by the time I reached my forties, the whole attitude of skeptical nihilism had become such an intrinsic part of my being, of my personality, that I paid it no more attention than my breathing or my pulse. The attitude was finally always 'there' accompanying me wherever I went. Moreover, I no longer felt lonely, depressed, or stressed out about not being able to explain my rare and unusual state of being to other people. So overall the process worked out beautifully for me. Nonetheless, those years of my life, roughly between the ages of 30 and 40, when the whole process had to work its way through my system, those were very difficult times."*

-- *"Then what came afterward?"*

-- *"Ha, well, afterward my life became much easier, at least in a material sense. I lived another several decades, became famous as an artist and a philosopher, and 'never looked back,' as they say down there."*

-- *"A happy ending then?"*

-- *"Yes, even a sense of triumph on the day I died. And now I'm back here in the higher realities, in the 'home' realities, helping prepare people like yourself for their series of visits to Earth."*

-- *"Well, it's time for me to go!"*

-- *"You'll forget this conversation, of course, but you will find me in symbols and signs throughout the Planet Earth reality. I also know your life will reach a conclusion of triumph much like mine did. Indeed, even if you cannot yet imagine it, I can already 'envision' that triumph, and what I 'see' is unbelievably beautiful, glorious, and uplifting. Take care* now!"

III.
Skeptical Nihilism And the Feast Of Creation

Contents

Editor's Introduction

The philosophical method and practice of skeptical nihilism, first published only as recently as 2014, is an outcome of one man's reasoning process over more than a decade and yet also represents the outcome of more than 400 years of Western intellectual history. That is to say, even while the man, Emericus Durden, developed the philosophy in relative privacy, it nonetheless bears the marks of many thinkers and philosophers who preceded him in Europe and North America.

This essay, the third Mr. Durden has written on the philosophical method, serves to place skeptical nihilism in the long-term historical context which gave rise to it, and to that extent, this essay is a scholarly exercise in the history of ideas rather than a primer or manual on the method itself. For the latter, the reader is referred to the author's *Aiming Higher Than Mere Civilization*.

By providing a historical context for Mr. Durden's philosophy, *Skeptical Nihilism And the Feast of Creation* strives to achieve a few things – first, it aims to show what methodological and theoretical features differentiate skeptical nihilism from the work of prior, better known skeptical philosophers such as Rene Descartes and Friedrich Nietzsche; second, it aims to show how the author's method builds on those prior philosophies, even boldly arguing that the method improves upon them; finally, the essay provides a basic summary of skeptical nihilism's goals on both the individual and social levels. To the extent those goals have not yet been achieved despite appearing nonetheless inevitable (to the author at least), the essay thus engages in an informal kind of soothsaying.

On that note, it's worth mentioning what's perhaps already obvious to an astute reader: in the scheme of things, Mr. Durden's skeptical nihilism occupies the crowning achievement of Western philosophical thought. While such a blatant teleological bias may seem wildly inappropriate for a genuine history of ideas (unless written by Hegel), it does in fact serve to show that the author intends to do more with this essay than simply offer a dispassionate recounting of historical facts.

Indeed, the essay also serves as a form of cultural critique, a fact that should come as no surprise to readers familiar with Mr. Durden's other work. Indeed, cultural criticism and polemic generally act as the background against which he prefers to explain the value of his philosophical method. In the particular instance of *Skeptical Nihilism And the Feast of Creation*, this criticism takes on a strong political flavor perhaps unavoidable given the deep influence of philosophical ideas on Western political history since the Renaissance.

On the other hand, the emphasis on politics may be somewhat surprising given that skeptical nihilism is first and foremost a psychological method designed to act directly on the mind of the individual, not a policy meant to address social ills and inequalities. However, the reader must keep in mind that a basic premise underlying the method is that psychological change drives social and political change, not vice versa. Thus, on Mr. Durden's view, voting and electoral politics by themselves are helpless to trigger lasting and substantial social change and should therefore be replaced by a program of substantial psychological change – admittedly, a point some readers may find rather disturbing.

Be that as it may, perhaps the most shocking, or at lest unconventional, aspect of this essay is its basic premise that the history of modern Western skeptical philosophy – spanning several centuries, from the times of Rene Descartes and the Enlightenment, through the 19th and 20th Centuries of Friedrich Nietzsche and postmodernism, finally to the current era of skeptical nihilism itself – is in fact a history of a prolonged and so far failed attempt to throw off the yoke of rationality and to unify humanity (or at least Western Civilization) under a unified, non-rational, transcendental perspective.

According to Mr. Durden's read on history, we (meaning Western philosophers, scientists, political leaders, or thinkers generally) have consistently sabotaged our own efforts to reach that transcendental perspective, for any number of reasons, in the process generating a social and political history characterized by endless and, in the author's view, fruitless back-and-forth battles between the two ideological camps of liberalism and conservatism.

In that historical context, Durden's skeptical nihilism, as the 'final' form of skeptical philosophy, becomes the definitive method for throwing off the yoke of rationality and finally delivering ourselves to the unified transcendental perspective we have for so long denied ourselves. Naturally, in the process of that delivery, not only does reason itself vanish in some manner, so do both liberalism and conservatism.

So what *is* this unified transcendental perspective and what purpose can it serve?

As for what the perspective *is* – well, Mr. Durden puts a fair amount of effort into discussing it both here and in his other two essays on skeptical nihilism (*Aiming Higher Than Mere Civilization* and *Beyond Words & Machines*). Nonetheless, he consistently runs up against the intrinsic difficulty of using language to describe a 'thing' that, by definition, is transcendental and therefore exists beyond words and other systems of representation. Clearly, the author understands this difficulty, accepting it without qualms, sometimes resorting to metaphors and analogies, other times using familiar words offset by quotation marks.

In any case, regarding the identity of the perspective, Mr. Durden's main point is that it must be *directly experienced*, not learned about through someone else's description of it. And a key goal of skeptical nihilism is to do exactly that: to 'introduce' the method's practitioner to this unified, transcendental perspective via direct experience. Having successfully done so, skeptical nihilism has no further purpose to serve and may, in some sense, be discarded.

As for the *purpose* of this unified, transcendental perspective – here we enter some rather interesting, even baffling, territory, which, I believe, is covered more thoroughly here in *Skeptical Nihilism And the Feast of Creation* than in the other two essays.

First of all, very much in the tradition of Cartesian metaphysics, Mr. Durden notes that the unified, transcendental perspective may serve as *a foundation and criterion of truth* for a new science and philosophy. Secondly, very much in the tradition of religious mysticism, he also notes that the same perspective (there can *be* only one such perspective, after all) may serve as *a gnosis experience of God* validating a new form of non-faith-based religion. Thirdly, very much in tradition of Western occult traditions and self-help gurus, he claims that the perspective may serve as *a stable basis for willed motivation and self-improvement*.

Taken together as a harmonious call to action, those three goals transform the individual's life into a 'feast of creation.' And in the case where many individuals reach this unified perspective, the implication is clear: civilization itself becomes a feast of creation.

I will leave it to the reader to decide whether or not Mr. Durden is merely the latest in a long line of naïve, utopian idealists who believe they possess *the* true recipe of peace, love, and understanding. In any case, this essay does provide a lot of material to ponder and critique in a relatively compressed space – and as an editor I certainly appreciate that.

Author's Introduction: Pursuit of the Truth and the Universal Dialogue of Reason

"If we want the door to turn, the hinges must stay put." – Ludwig Wittgenstein, On Certainty

A pursuit of the truth, as opposed to a pursuit of happiness, led me to the insights underlying the philosophical method of skeptical nihilism. While there is nothing, so far as I can tell, requiring truth and happiness to be mutually exclusive, in my life the two generally have been so. Moreover, I believe each of those pursuits has a very different set of ethical and political implications, and skeptical nihilism reflects those differences.

What do I mean by 'the truth' anyway? Well, I mean 'that which is eternal' or 'that which is unchanging.' When we recognize that everything *evident* around us is, in fact, impermanent and always changing, we also recognize that, by my definition, ***a pursuit of the truth is necessarily a pursuit of something non-evident***.

In contrast to a pursuit of the truth thus defined, a pursuit of happiness, as commonly understood, is a pursuit of something 'pleasurable' or 'enjoyable,' of identifiable sensations associated with feelings of satisfaction – that is, *a pursuit of happiness is a pursuit of something evident*.

Presumably all of my readers have pursued, discovered, and enjoyed evident things that bring happiness, but how can any of us ever hope to discover something non-evident, something imperceptible and undetectable? Is that not the very definition of a fool's errand? Well, in fact, the way to achieve the latter is surprisingly easy to state if, in fact, incredibly difficult to accomplish in practice – namely, we must cast aside all things evident, and what remains, *if* anything remains, can only be the non-evident.

But how do we 'cast aside all things evident'? Well, we subject the existence of those evident things to doubt and skepticism, which is to say, we ask of each of those things, "Must this thing exist in all times and all places, or is this thing's existence contingent on a particular place and time?" When the latter statement holds, we may conclude that the evident thing we are doubting is in fact contingent, therefore not eternal, and thus we may cast it aside in our pursuit of the truth.

In this manner, we may systematically proceed to doubt all of our sensations, thoughts, ideas, beliefs, and theories, from our earliest childhood to the present day – in short, we may doubt everything we've ever perceived, thought, felt, learned, or believed, *including doubt itself*. And after that long, arduous process, if anything at all remains standing, it must be something true and non-evident.

The truth thus discovered is ***certain*** because it necessarily withstands all tests of doubt. It is ***eternal*** because it necessarily withstands all tests of contingency. In the sense it exists 'outside' or 'beyond' our evident world, the truth thus discovered is necessarily ***transcendental***. Moreover, by virtue of being eternal and transcendental, this discovered truth is a ***unity***. Finally, to the extent this truth is 'metaphysically prior' to the evident world of change and contingency, we may assert it is ***a condition*** of the latter or, at the very least, ***a foundation***.

The previous several paragraphs describing the pursuit of the truth also describe, in broad outline, the method of skeptical nihilism. Thus, ***the method serves to identify a truth that is certain, eternal, transcendental, unified and that may serve as a condition or foundation of the evident world of change and contingency. This truth is a direct, unmediated experience, not a proposition, a statement of fact, or an attitude of faith.***

Indeed, to ensure that the truth so discovered is certain and eternal, each individual must directly experience it and know it for himself, not merely taking someone else's word for its existence. In other words, each individual must embark on his own pursuit of the truth rather than appoint one person do it who then reports back his findings to the wider community. This should be obvious given that the latter situation requires belief (or faith) in that one seeker's claims, which are naturally susceptible to skeptical doubt based on any number of contingent factors.

So there you have it – the pursuit of the truth and its codification in the method of skeptical nihilism.

Now, does that method prevail or even exist today in society, in civilization? I would argue it does not exist except among a few rare oddballs like myself, Emericus Durden. In its place, we have two other activities: a pursuit of happiness, briefly described above, and what I call the universal dialogue of reason. As I will show in Part I below, those two activities derive directly from the European Enlightenment tradition and have given rise to the two prevailing and competing political ideologies of our age, liberalism and conservatism.

If the reader is paying close attention here, he might ask, "So do you mean to imply that liberalism and conservatism do not take part in the pursuit of the truth?"

"Indeed, they do not," I would reply, "at least not in the way I define the truth. Instead, those two political ideologies take part in the universal dialogue of reason."

On my view, the universal dialogue of reason is society's collective activity of comparing, contrasting, analyzing, and synthesizing the opinions, beliefs, theories, and ideologies that have circulated throughout our communities from time immemorial. Some version of it has probably existed for as long as human societies have existed. But what interests me here is the current version of this dialogue, which derives from the ideas of 17th and 18th Century European philosophers.

It is my contention that ever so gradually over the past three-hundred or so years, the universal dialogue of reason, as I've described it above, has crowded out the pursuit of the truth to such an extent that even common sense now argues against the possibility of a non-evident, eternal, unified transcendental truth, not to mention the actual existence thereof.

Instead of a pursuit of the truth, the universal dialogue of reason has delivered us to world of diverse, conflicting opinions, ceaseless debate and argumentation, social and ethnic chaos, all in the context of a relativistic understanding of the truth which accepts contingency and randomness as unavoidable facts of human life and rejects even the possibility of the existence of anything eternal that all human beings share. In short, the universal dialogue of reason has delivered us to the worlds of relativism and liberalism.

"But isn't that a good thing?" the reader might ask. "Aren't liberalism's freedom of expression and the universal rights of man examples of progress and advancement over universal ignorance conditioned by tyranny and religious faith?"

"To that extent, and only to that extent, liberalism is a good thing," I would reply. "For the liberal impulse did ultimately abolish the power of the church and the rule of kings and emperors. Nonetheless, since that time, liberalism has failed miserably to unite diverse people and opinions under common experiences and common knowledge. In place of that unity, an undercurrent of social tension, conflict, and incipient chaos runs through our liberal societies, leading desperate and confused people to develop extreme beliefs based, for example, on race and religion, which, they foolishly hope, will bring order to their chaotic lives. Instead, those extreme beliefs trigger only more conflict, more social chaos, more fear and hatred."

"So," the reader might ask, "if I understand you correctly, you're saying that liberalism, in some form or other, is directly responsible for the extreme racist and religious ideologies circulating in our world?"

"Indeed, that's the implication, and the process works like this: first, liberalism's universal dialogue of reason breeds ideological uncertainty, conflict, and chaos. Next, in an attempt to quell that uncertainty and chaos, some desperate individuals resort to extreme ideologies like religious fundamentalism and racism. However, those extreme ideologies inevitably trigger opposition, which further escalates the uncertainty and chaos rather than reducing it. Finally, in the worst case scenario, that opposition transforms itself into outright war."

Clearly, then, my political motive or purpose behind the method of skeptical nihilism is **to bring unity to a highly fractured society by allowing each person to uniquely experience the one eternal truth we all share in our human diversity**. Indeed, only when a great diversity of people directly experiences and shares in their knowledge of the 'same' eternal truth can they describe their society as a 'unity in diversity.'

On this view, then, the overarching philosophical and political position of liberalism remains important though only as one historical step or stage on our journey toward skeptical nihilism. In other words, liberalism and its universal dialogue of reason must serve as a means to an end rather than as an end in themselves.

In the following section, I trace the development of Western skeptical philosophy from Rene Descartes to the present day. Along the way, we'll see how the interplay between liberal and reactionary (conservative) philosophical ideals has paved the way for the ultimate arrival of skeptical nihilism.

Part I: No-Saying: The Freedom To Think For Oneself

The Lord said to Satan, "From where have you come?" Satan answered the Lord and said, "From going to and fro on the earth, and from walking up and down on it." – Job 1:7

The first 'thing' that happens to any human being at any moment in the their lives is the perception that *everything is changing*. The second 'thing' that happens to any human being at any moment in their lives is the question, *But is there anything unchanging, anything permanent, eternal, absolute?* The third 'thing' that *may* happen to any human at any moment in their lives is the decision *to discover something unchanging amid everything that's changing.*

The person who goes off seeking the unchanging amid the changing is known as the 'skeptic.' **He seeks the truth in the answer to the question, Does anything unchanging, anything eternal exist?** He may find the answer is 'yes' or 'no' or he may find nothing to support either answer and suspend judgment on the matter. Those are his three basic options. In any case, his is a quest for direct knowledge, direct experience of the eternal truth, not merely evidence to support a belief or faith in its existence. Clearly, the skeptic is an individual on an private quest. However, when society as a whole embarks on a search for an answer to that question, the result is a collective quest in search of the eternal truth which, over time, may eventually give rise to what we call 'civilization.'

The skeptic begins his quest facing, as it were, what is immediately given him every moment of his life: the perceptions of his five senses and the thoughts and feelings triggered by those perceptions – such is the evidence supporting the phrase 'everything is changing.' The tool the skeptic uses to sort through what is changing to discover what is eternal (if it exists) is called 'reason' or 'rationality.' As the skeptic gropes his way forward, applying reason to his senses, thoughts, and beliefs, rationally investigating his perceptual and mental realities, comparing, contrasting, analyzing, criticizing what he learns, all in pursuit of the eternal truth, his activity gives rise to those spheres of knowledge comprising humanity's cultural achievements: the arts, the humanities, science and engineering, religion, commerce, and statecraft.

However, time introduces a wrinkle into the skeptic's quest.

The skeptic slowly, insidiously drifts away from his original goal of finding what's eternal and increasingly focuses on his cultural achievements as ends in themselves rather than as means to discovering the truth. Generation upon generation of seekers and skeptics, thus 'going to and fro on the earth,' 'walking up and down on it,' eventually results in a civilization that celebrates those cultural achievements, describing them as 'advancement' and 'innovation,' without suspecting they may be little more than distractions from humanity's highest goal: finding the eternal truth. Indeed, that goal may eventually seem ridiculous and naïve, hardly worthy of serious human endeavor, and therefore best consigned to the category of delusion.

In such a civilization, where the spheres of knowledge and their accompanying achievements are celebrated as self-standing pursuits, skeptics become confined to this or that discipline, exercising their skeptical reasoning abilities only within the narrow limits of the rules of a single intellectual realm. Consequently, those skeptics become dogmatists, often without realizing it, presuming the superiority of their discipline over the others (for example, proclaiming the superiority of the scientific method over religious faith).

Ultimately, this fracturing of the quest for the eternal truth into a great many competing pursuits for dogmatic knowledge results in a civilization that even behaves 'unreasonably' or 'irrationally' relative to the skeptic's original goal of finding the truth. Even worse, such an irrational civilization may continue to consider itself rational despite displaying the most irrational tendencies.

Nonetheless, there's a silver lining to this cloud, for at that point of self-contradiction when civilization is unable or unwilling to admit it has locked itself into a prison of irrationality and dogmatism it nonetheless insists is rational – at *that* point, the time is ripe for reason to refute itself, to wipe itself out, as it were, and in so doing, miraculously, to deliver humanity to its original goal: the eternal truth: the unchanging amid the changing.

Thus, we arrive at one of the great paradoxes, enacted on the level of both individual lives and entire civilizations: *only when we've drifted furthest off course have we in fact come nearest to our highest goal: finding the eternal truth.*

The author believes we have indeed arrived at this great paradox today, in the early 21st Century – which is to say the time is ripe for reason to refute itself and deliver us into the 'arms' of the eternal truth. The purpose of skeptical nihilism, as is made clear below, is to accelerate and enhance that delivery.

However, before we discuss the ultimate outcome of skeptical nihilism, I believe it's important to consider the last time our civilization arrived at the same great paradox and what followed. By understanding the prior outcome, we will not only better understand what led us to our present predicament, we will also better appreciate what lies ahead for all of us.

a. Enter Rene Descartes

The last time civilization reached a paradoxical juncture was during the 16th and 17th Centuries, when a civilization beset by the irrationalities of monarchy and church dogma nonetheless insisted on its own rational foundations. Clearly disturbed by this self-contradictory state of affairs even if not stating it exactly in those terms, the French philosopher Rene Descartes developed a method suitable to his times that might clear up the contradiction and clarify, at least to himself, what is true and what is false, what is doubtful and what is certain in human life.

While he obviously didn't call his method 'skeptical nihilism,' in broad outline it is a clear precursor to my modern method. Like skeptical nihilism, Descartes' method harnessed the destructive powers of reason to wipe out all 'false opinions' in an attempt to identify the one thing that is certain, true, and eternally beyond doubt, *if* such a thing exists. Having found such an indestructible 'thing,' Descartes might then use it as a foundation on which to build a new understanding of nature and society and perhaps even a new civilization no longer beset by the self-contradictory claims of tyrannical authorities.

Thus, in his *Meditations on First Philosophy* (1641), Descartes describes his intentions to "devote myself, in sober earnest and with entire freedom, to the business of destroying all my former opinions," "withdrawing myself from everything in which I can imagine the least doubt, just as if I knew it to be absolutely false; and shall keep steadily on in this path until I have found something certain..."

Application of the above method to the contents of his own mind over the period of a few days led Descartes "to hold for certain that this proposition - *I am, I exist* - is necessarily true" and therefore to conclude that the proposition may serve as the foundation for his new science. (In other contexts he states the same proposition more famously as *I think, therefore I am*.)

In summary, then, Descartes first proceeds analytically (by application of systematic doubt) to identify truths that are 'clear and distinct' ideas. Then, having identified such a truth ("I think, therefore I am"), he uses it as a foundation on which to build (by logical deduction) the complex propositions comprising human knowledge. In conclusion, Descartes believes he has shown, among other things, that reason is capable of separating false opinions from eternal truth.

While abstract in its initial presentation, Descartes' method of using reason to wipe out false opinions to arrive at 'clear and distinct' ideas was adapted by many other philosophers in the ensuing century, leading up to and including the era of the European Enlightenment.

As one example of the method's practical consequences, consider how British philosopher John Locke used the same mode of reasoning to identify the 'nature of man' [i.e., nature of human beings] as well as the form of government most compatible with that nature: "a state of perfect freedom to order [humanity's] actions and dispose of their possessions and persons ... within the bounds of the laws of nature. A state also of equality..." (*Two Treatises of Government* (1689)).

Based on that description of government, arrived at entirely by Locke's use of an abstract reasoning process, Thomas Jefferson rationalized the abolition of British rule over the Colonies, stating in the *Declaration of Independence* (1776) that it was acceptable to overturn any form of government that failed to secure self-evident truths (equality) and certain unalienable rights (life, liberty, pursuit of happiness). Similar reasoning would be used to support the French Revolution a decade later.

We see, then, how Descartes' method of skeptical reasoning cast doubt on and irrevocably damaged categories of traditional European political governance - monarch, emperor, king, prince, priest, pope – by revealing they were out of harmony with the 'nature of man,' and thus made way for their replacement with entirely new categories like Jeffersonian democracy.

Now let's step back for a moment and ask, But did Descartes' method actually arrive at its stated goal – to find that which is beyond all doubt and uncertainty, i.e., to find the eternal truth: that which is unchanging amid the changing?

As we'll see a below, skeptical nihilism answers that question with an unequivocal 'no.' While it's clear Descartes made a partially successful first attempt to clear away all false opinions, he nonetheless left a few contingent 'beliefs' standing. Indeed, we hardly to need to wait for the arrival of skeptical nihilism to prove this point, as a number of thinkers in the 18th and 19th Centuries already answered 'no' to the above question. The main target of those thinkers' criticism was Descartes' belief in 'clear and distinct' ideas. Responding to the results of Descartes' reason, they asked, But do such clear and distinct ideas have an existence outside the mind? Do they occur anywhere in the world of our senses? Do they occur anywhere in history? Are they even *real*? *Are they eternally true?*

Most famously, French philosopher Joseph de Maistre (1797) in his *Considerations on France*, asked whether it makes sense even to proclaim the eternal truth of concepts like 'the nature of man' and 'the rights of man,' when, in fact, "there is no such thing in the world as *man*. In my life I have seen Frenchmen, Italians, Russians, and so on. I even know, thanks to Montesquieu, that one can be Parisian. But as for man, I declare I've never encountered him. If he exists, I don't know about it."

Indeed, many thinkers throughout the 19th Century interpreted the evidence of history and social science as a direct refutation of the eternal truth of Descartes' clear and distinct ideas.

Thus, philosopher Arthur Gobineau in his now notorious *The Inequality of Human Races* (1853), stated that "no one can claim any longer to explain the complicated play of social forces, the causes of the rise and decay of nations, in the light of the purely abstract and hypothetical arguments supplied by [Descartes'] skeptical philosophy. Since we have now an abundance of positive facts crowding upon us from all sides, ... we may no longer, like the theorists of the [French] Revolution, form a collection of imaginary beings out of clouds. ... *There is only one tribunal competent to decide rationality upon the general characteristics of man, and that is history...*"[italics mine].

But some philosophers dug deeper, questioning much more than Descartes' clear and distinct ideas, indeed, casting doubt on the eternal validity of the Cartesian reasoning process itself. Most famously, British philosopher David Hume's analysis of reason led him to conclude that it is impossible to make the sorts of logical deductions Descartes' method does without relying on the contingent habits of human perception, which is to say, without relying on some form of social tradition not much different from the religious traditions Descartes and other Enlightenment figures were trying to decimate using reason.

b. Enter Friedrich Nietzsche

While the German Enlightenment tradition of Kant and Hegel went to great lengths to answer Hume's criticism and thus, in some technical sense, save Descartes' project, even the various Kantian and neo-Kantian projects were not immune to the most scathing of all critics of Descartes' project: Friedrich Nietzsche. Expanding on those prior criticisms, Nietzsche finally landed the deathblow to Cartesian metaphysics, developing the outlines of a philosophy that would later be variously called 'perspectivism,' 'epistemological relativism,' and 'nihilism.'

While famous for declaring the death of God, in fact Nietzsche did far more than that: he declared the death of truth or, to put it more cryptically though still accurately, he declared the ascendency of lies masquerading as truth.

As Nietzsche states in *Ecce Homo* (1888), "All the things men have valued with such earnestness heretofore are not even realities; they are mere fantasies, or, more strictly speaking, lies arising from the evil instincts of diseased and, in the deepest sense, harmful natures - all the concepts, 'God,' 'soul,' 'virtue,' 'sin,' 'Beyond,' 'truth,' 'eternal life.'" And further in the same book: "Everything that has hitherto been called 'truth' has been recognized as the most harmful, insidious, and subterranean form of lie... Whoever uncovers morality also uncovers the disvalue of all values that are and have been believed ..."

But if what Nietzsche states is indeed the case, what then becomes of reason, of ethics, indeed, of the entire edifice of philosophy and science? Well, Nietzsche provided one answer early in his career, in the essay "On

Truth and Lies in the Extra-Moral Sense" (1873), where he states that "to be truthful means to employ the usual metaphors. Thus, to express it morally, this is the duty to lie according to a fixed convention, to lie with the herd and in a manner binding upon everyone." In other words, Nietzsche replaces eternal truth with the conventions of artistic expression, which apparently leaves nothing non-contingent and eternal in its wake, nothing unchanging amid all that is changing.

Now let us step back and assess the situation.

Some two-hundred-and-fifty years have elapsed between Descartes' publication of his skeptical reasoning method and Nietzsche's nihilism. Over that time, we have seen the rise of the European Enlightenment and political movements like the American and French Revolutions, as well as subsequent reactions to those movements throughout the 19th Century.

And what can we conclude? Well, it seems that **in the figure of Friedrich Nietzsche the process of skeptical reasoning first unleashed by Descartes to ferret out 'false opinions' has finally turned back on itself and declared itself a false opinion**, refuting itself outright, applying its own destructive methods to its own universal categories – 'truth,' 'reality,' 'freedom,' 'equality' – and thus, in some sense, revealing the emptiness of those categories and of itself, leaving us finally adrift in a sea of relativism, contingency, and randomness.

Thus, the very the method of skeptical reasoning that helped rescue civilization from the absolutism and tyranny of monarchs, emperors, and popes, would seem finally to abandon us to a world where only relative truths exist, where social conflict and ethnic violence seem to lurk around every corner, where, in some strange sense, nihilism is considered acceptable amid endless calls from leaders for 'tolerance' and 'compassion' – in short, abandoned us to the worldview called 'liberalism.'

But must this liberalism, this epistemological relativism be the inevitable outcome of Descartes' skeptical reasoning process? Or are we perhaps giving up too soon, forgetting that Nietzsche's worldview of nihilism and its implied liberal chaos may be merely another historical stage on our way to achieving humanity's highest goal: finding the eternal truth, the unchanging amid the changing?

This essay's position is clear: Nietzsche's nihilism, for all its destructive force, is indeed merely another stage along the way and therefore not the endgame, not a cul-de-sac, certainly not a state of terminal meaninglessness – more precisely, it is the penultimate stage which can lead, if we allow it to evolve and transform itself, into the final stage of skeptical nihilism.

But before I discuss that final stage, I will briefly address the various ideological barriers that continue to delay our progress, holding us hostage to nihilism and liberalism, preventing civilization from making that final transition to skeptical nihilism. Understanding those barriers is important because it helps illustrate why this book didn't arrive on the scene sooner, indeed, as much as one-hundred years sooner, had Nietzsche (or his followers) been willing to explore, embrace, and *directly experience* the full implications of his brand of nihilism.

All we have to do is look at the history of the 19th and 20th Centuries to see how time and again philosophers and political thinkers, rather than working out the full implications of Nietzsche's nihilism, instead attempted to block and even roll back the skeptical reasoning process that logically led them to it. In its place, they attempted to erect this or that ideological framework (what I call an 'idol of permanence') to serve, they hoped, as a source of unity and stability in a world perceived to be filled with liberal chaos and conflict.

And what was the result of those idols of permanence? Don't take my word for it – look for yourself: two world wars, a depression, a cold war, and a war on terror. In other words, repeated attempts to block the development of liberal chaos has merely resulted in still more conflict and chaos. This point helps explain why I am equally critical of liberalism and conservatism. The former inadvertently creates social chaos, and the latter, in an attempt to combat and prevent that chaos, inadvertently creates still more conflict and chaos. Thus, liberalism and conservatism are equally complicit in the warlike, competitive mentality that now reigns and is considered 'normal' in today's world.

In the 19th Century, a central 'idol of permanence' fashioned by conservative thinkers to prevent liberal chaos was the concept of 'race.' Here the idea was to use evidence from history and the social sciences to identify a superior race, based on genetic and behavioral features, which could appoint itself to lead all of humanity into a future of peace and eternal truth. Thus, in complete opposition to the spirit of Descartes' skeptical reasoning, Gobineau stated "there are real differences in the relative value of human races" and then used those differences to argue against a notion like 'all men are created equal.'

But to be fair, conservative thinkers have not been the only ones attempting to block the skeptical reasoning process. Indeed, in parallel with the concept of race, the 19th Century saw the rise of another 'idol of permanence,' the concept of 'class,' developed by Karl Marx, who to this day is a poster-boy for various forms of moderate to extreme liberalism. (How this association came about is somewhat complex and not a topic for this book.)

Much like races, the existence of economic classes was argued based on the evidence of history and social sciences, not based on a process of pure skeptical reasoning. Also like race, one class was considered superior to the others and thus appointed to be the driving force of history, leading all of humanity into the glorious future.

Of course, we only have to look at mid-20th-Century Europe to appreciate the 'glorious' future delivered to humanity by anti-skeptical concepts like 'race' and 'class.'

The important point for us is this: 'race' and 'class' found enthusiastic support among certain nations and peoples only at the severe cost of their ignoring the implications of the Cartesian/Nietzschean skeptical tradition. Indeed, I believe it's safe to say that neither of those two thinkers would have associated himself with concepts like 'race' and 'class.' Descartes would have called them both false opinions that failed to meet his criterion of clear and distinct ideas, while Nietzsche would have derided them both as empty lies no different from similar lies like 'God' and 'eternal life.'

Thus, I can only conclude that two-hundred-and-fifty years of skeptical reasoning by brilliant thinkers could have prevented, at least in theory, the rise of 20th Century totalitarianism had European leaders only embraced the full implications of that skeptical reasoning process and founded their governing policies on those implications rather than on idols of permanence like race and class. Alas, it didn't work out that way.

Meanwhile, even with 20th Century totalitarianism and fascism behind us, we still have failed to understand and move forward with the skeptical reasoning project, much less move beyond and transcend it (as skeptical nihilism advocates). Instead, we have resigned ourselves to a world where relativistic, chaotic liberalism is *supposedly* the cost of the Enlightenment tradition that gave rise to the American and French Revolutions, the industrial revolution, and modern-day economic globalization.

Indeed, in much of Western academia, this type of 'late-day' liberalism is embraced under the banners of 'postmodernism' and 'post-structuralism,' and often celebrated as a form of intellectual common sense.

Thus, American philosopher Richard Rorty in his *Contingency, Irony, and Solidarity* (1989) states that society's interests might best be served "by ceasing to see truth as a deep matter, as a topic of philosophical interest, or 'true' as a term which repays 'analysis.' 'The nature of truth' is an unprofitable topic. ... But this claim about relative profitability, in turn, is just the recommendation that we in fact *say* little about these topics, and see how we get on."

Rorty's ultimate goal is "to get to the point where we no longer worship *anything*, where we treat *nothing* as a quasi divinity, where we treat *everything* – our language, our conscience, our community – as a product of time and chance."

While Nietzsche would likely have agreed with the basic gist of these comments, it's doubtful he would have been satisfied with the sense of powerlessness over reality they convey.

In contrast to Rorty's playful if perhaps naïve optimism, a second group of thinkers, stretching back to the Second World War, if not a bit earlier, have simply resigned themselves to the nihilism intrinsic to the liberal project, noting that the accompanying technological efficiencies created by skeptical reasoning may preserve order in society, even if at the steep cost of a mechanization of social relations.

Thus, German philosopher Max Horkheimer in his 1941 essay "The End of Reason" states that, even while Descartes' rationalistic metaphysics may be a thing of the past, "the patterns of rationalistic behavior remain. ... Its features can be summarized as the optimum adaptation of means to ends ... It is a pragmatic instrument oriented to expediency, cold and sober."

Unfortunately, that rational expediency pushed too far inevitably leads society into another self-contradictory impasse of irrationality. As Oswald Spengler pointed out in his *Man And Technology* (1931), civilization becomes "a machine that does, or tries to do, everything in mechanical fashion. We think only in horse-power now; we cannot look at a waterfall without mentally turning it into electric power; we cannot survey a countryside of pasturing cattle without thinking of its exploitation as a source of meat-supply."

c. Enter Emericus Durden

Stepping back now and surveying the history of ideas from Descartes' 17th Century to our present day, we note that a series of intellectual 'barriers' or, changing the metaphor, a gallery of hypnotic 'idols' has repeatedly kept Descartes' skeptical reasoning process from reaching its ultimate end.

The result has been, on the one hand, a liberal political philosophy that upholds universal human rights at the cost of chronic, underlying social tensions and conflicts, and, on the other hand, a series of conservative reactions to that philosophy expressed by various forms of fundamentalism or, even worse, social, political, and economic repression.

We find ourselves living in a civilization that reflects a broad diversity of conflicting cultural opinions without any kind of overarching political or social unity.

Now, a great many people would say that, although the situation is not ideal, it's more or less the best we can do at this point in history, and anyway, we should be highly suspicious of any attempt to unify humanity under an ideological or philosophical banner. That suspicion is founded on two basic premises – one, that empirical science finds no evidence of a unifying factor among human beings beyond trivial, biological features like the necessity to breathe, and two, that world history shows many horrific examples of how attempts to mobilize and unify large numbers of people result in extreme forms of political repression as witnessed in Nazi Germany and Soviet Russia or in horrific forms of terror like Islamic fundamentalism.

There's no denying the above two points. However, we do ourselves a great disservice if we conclude from them that there is no way to unify our social diversity. Rather, we would do ourselves a greater service to limit our conclusion to this statement: unifying humanity based on empirical properties or historically conditioned belief systems will not work without morally unacceptable forms of repression and violence. I certainly agree with that statement.

But then I ask you (in rather abstract fashion), ***Might we not unify human diversity based on each individual's unique experience of a shared non-evident property?*** Indeed, if there's one theme sorely lacking in much of the history of skeptical reasoning as I've outlined it, from Descartes to Nietzsche, it's the theme of non-evident features or properties.

So what do I mean by a non-evident property? Well, of course, this brings us back to the pursuit of the eternal truth which underlies skeptical nihilism.

A non-evident property is something we cannot detect with our five senses or, by implication, with any scientific instrumentation. Fair enough. But do we have any words in our language that refer to non-evident properties? In fact, we do have such words: 'eternal truth,' 'mind,' 'consciousness,' 'soul,' 'spirit,' 'God,' 'transcendence,' among others.

Now, according to empirical science and logical semantics, those words refer to something that does not exist, and according to mainstream religions, those words refer to something that does exist but that we can only have faith in, not direct knowledge of. For the time being, we shall put aside the conclusions of science and religion.

Returning to what I stated above, I now rephrase my question as follows: ***Might we not unify human diversity based on each individual's direct knowledge of a unifying, non-evident property like 'spirit,' 'truth,' or 'transcendence'?***

Here skeptical nihilism enters the picture.

Taking up Descartes' skeptical reasoning process where Nietzsche left off with it, skeptical nihilism moves one step further and answers the above question in the affirmative: *the method of skeptical nihilism demonstrates it is possible for each and every individual to have direct knowledge of **transcendence***: a *real* experience, a *direct* experience, a *practical, private*, even highly *political* experience.

As such, skeptical nihilism refuses to accept a world of diversity without unity. Instead, it pushes the skeptical urge still further forward, casting doubt on all past, present, and potential belief systems, *including itself*, finally pushing the thinker's mind beyond logical reasoning itself, beyond all systems of representation, to the very breaking point of paradox, forcing the mind to be skeptical about skepticism, to doubt 'doubt.' Only afterwards, in the rubble of such logical self-refutation, does the thinker directly experience the only 'thing' that remains: transcendence: the '***unchanging*** amid the changing,' 'the ***certain*** amid the doubtful': 'the ***non-evident perspective***' which all human beings everywhere, in all ages and places, share, the one 'thing' forever beyond their doubt having experienced it just once.

Thus achieving transcendence amid the ruins of reason, we learn directly that the unifying, non-evident property of transcendence serves as the necessary condition for reason and the empirical world in which it operates. A such, the transcendental perspective is logically independent of all doubt and skepticism, eternally secure in its certainty, enjoying direct authority over the world of our senses.

On a moral level, each human being also discovers that indeed something 'higher' exists, unifying all human activity even while allowing each human being to affirm his or her uniqueness. Moreover, by its very existence as the condition of our daily world, that higher 'thing' logically compels the humility of humanity while also inspiring the compassion of each human being for his or her fellow man and woman.

So let's step back and take stock of what we've learned about skeptical nihilism's transcendental outcome.

First, there is *the spiritual outcome of skeptical nihilism*: to 'liberate' individuals from the contingencies of their personal beliefs and opinions, their emotions, their very own personalities, thus 'introducing' them to a unified transcendence shared by all human beings. In so doing, skeptical nihilism demonstrates that each human being is, in fact, a ***transcendental awareness*** existing independently of biology, language, and all social and cultural traditions.

Second, there is *the philosophical and scientific outcome of skeptical nihilism*: to 'introduce' individuals to unified transcendence as the criterion or standard of truth, enabling them to have direct, incontrovertible knowledge of something eternal and unchanging. In so doing, skeptical nihilism grants each human being direct knowledge of ***a higher reality*** that serves as a condition and a foundation for humanity's relative truths and therefore also as a unity amid the irreducible diversity of our ever changing, impermanent world.

Third, there is *the religious outcome of skeptical nihilism*: to 'introduce' individuals to unified transcendence as a direct experience of divinity, enabling them to experience gnosis or mystical union with a higher being. In so doing, skeptical nihilism grants each human being ***union with God***, no longer requiring him to rely on a faith in the teachings of religious authorities and prophets.

Fourth, there is *the ethical and political outcome of skeptical nihilism*: to 'introduce' individuals to unified transcendence as a detached perspective onto humanity, enabling them to rise above liberalism's universal dialogue of reason and conservatism's dogmatic fundamentalism. In so doing, skeptical nihilism grants each human being ***a transcendental perspective*** that 'sees' the unity of humanity in all of its irreducible diversity.

The above four *non-evident* outcomes – transcendental awareness, a higher reality, union with God, and a transcendental perspective – are the initial fruits of undertaking and successfully completing the practice of skeptical nihilism. None of those outcomes is predicted by empirical science (biology, chemistry, physics). Indeed, science denies those outcomes even exist. Moreover, established religions (Christianity, Judaism, Islam) declare those outcomes heretical.

Thus, in the current scheme of things, skeptical nihilism would seem to deliver its practitioners to experiences that are unacceptable, even unimaginable to the so-called 'experts.' We would all be wise to keep that point uppermost in our minds as we apply ourselves to this work.

Finally, there is one other outcome of skeptical nihilism, the most practical, the most important outcome of them all: *the artistic outcome of skeptical nihilism*: to 'introduce' individuals to unified transcendence as the basis on which to envision and materialize daily life itself. The second and final section of the essay is devoted to this outcome.

Part II: Yes-Saying: The Feast of Creation

"I must Create a System, or be enslav'd by another Man's. I will not Reason & Compare; my business is to Create." – William Blake, Jerusalem, the Emanation of the Giant Albion

Now that we've successfully used skeptical nihilism to deliver ourselves to a state of unified transcendence, now that we've achieved direct knowledge of truth, God, and transcendental awareness and freed ourselves from both dogma and criticism, our old habits of skeptical reasoning, of investigating and analyzing reality, no longer hold much value for us because they have served their purpose. We are thus no longer compelled to practice skeptical nihilism, and placing it aside, we ask ourselves, *But what is there left to do in this life?* (Simply holding down a job, earning a living, marrying, and raising a family were always beneath us anyway.)

In a word, what's left to do is this: ***create***. We have now earned the privilege to become visionaries and creators. Daily life itself becomes our creative art. This final stage I describe as the 'feast of creation.'

We must now pause and consider how significantly this stage differs from everything we have achieved leading up to it. First and foremost, this stage exists 'beyond' all forms of criticism (including skeptical nihilism itself), beyond all concerns with 'right' and 'wrong,' with 'true' and 'false.' At this stage we put aside our critical intelligence forever because it no longer has any value to us.

It's only natural that we find this new state of affairs disturbing, at least at first, given how intensely we previously focused on using our skeptical intelligence to achieve the non-evident outcome of eternal truth. But that's all in the past. We must now acclimate ourselves to an existence where ***willed imagination***, not skeptical reasoning, becomes the centerpiece of our existence. We must learn to thrive in a world where 'yes' reigns supreme and 'no' is rarely if ever spoken.

We are now creators, no longer critics and skeptics. Our commitment is to ***constructive creation***, not to destructive criticism. Thus, we must be forever on guard never to fall back into our old skeptical habits, which would only damage and destroy the very world we are trying to create through our imaginations.

So how does this all work? Well, it works the only way creation can ever work – *consciously*. That is to say, we use our imaginations to consciously envision the world we want live in. Then we consciously choose the beliefs that support and are congruent with that envisioned world. Finally, we focus our inner energy on those beliefs and the accompanying vision, which, by the transcendental laws of reality, must eventually materialize in the outer world of matter.

Such is the essence of creation – certainly something easier said than done.

Now the astute (and probably impatient) reader might ask, "Okay, that's all well and good, but couldn't we do this creation right off the bat, without first embarking on that long, tortuous journey of skeptical reasoning and skeptical nihilism?"

"Well, you could certainly *try*," I answer. "But the point of all that prior work is to ensure that by the time you reach this stage, you are qualified to become a creator. In order for creation to be effective, you need a stable, unchanging foundation from which to envision your life and choose your beliefs. As I've shown above, skeptical nihilism delivers you just such a stable, unchanging foundation: the eternal truth. That's why you go through the skeptical reasoning process first: to give yourself the proper basis from which to create."

"But could I create without such a basis?"

"As I said before, you could certainly *try* – and anyway, in some sense, you and everyone else is already creating without such a basis, you just don't realize it. As a result, the lifestyles and societies you are creating are unstable, chaotic, always in a state of apparently random flux. If that's what you want, then perhaps you don't need my lessons. But is it what you want? I doubt it, otherwise you wouldn't be here. So again I emphasize that we go through skeptical nihilism 'training' simply to ensure you have the best chance of becoming a strong, energetic, stable creator."

Based on the foregoing, we may now draw the three central conclusions of this essay, which also serve to unite Parts I and II:

First, ***becoming a creator means being in total control of one's imagination and beliefs***.

Second, ***beliefs are what ultimately matter in how we create our lives, not data or evidence***.

Third, ***the purpose of skeptical reason is to directly experience a stable, unchanging, transcendental foundation on which to base our creation: the eternal truth***.

Before reading this essay, you might have thought that a belief is merely a string of words spoken or written down that could just as well be disposed of at one's whim or based on this or that piece of evidence. In other words, before reading this book, you might have had the following 'belief about beliefs': beliefs are merely verbalized interpretations of the world.

But now, as an initial exercise in belief modification, I suggest you discard the above belief about beliefs, replacing it with this belief: *beliefs are the tools by which we create the world.*

By now it should be obvious that the final stage of this entire process – the stage I'm calling the feast of creation – is indeed the most mysterious of all the stages. Why? Because its very premise contradicts expert (science) and layman (common sense) alike.

In this day and age, we have certain beliefs that are so ingrained, so 'obvious' to us, we never even put them into words. One of those beliefs is that randomness reigns throughout the universe. Not only do the theories of most scientists unquestionably accept that belief, but the common sense we use everyday to interpret our world also embraces it.

Yet we should know better – indeed, if we've read and understood this essay, we *do* know better. We know, first, that 'randomness reigns throughout the universe' is a belief, and, second, we know that as a belief it may be subjected to the same skeptical doubt as any other belief, shown to be contingent, and thus discarded like any other belief.

Having discarded that belief, we are faced with a world, a universe where randomness no longer exists, where everything has a purpose, a plan. Moreover, it's *your* plan, designed according to your abilities to envision your future and put into action by your will. So let's face the brutal reality of the facts at hand: manifesting your will, creating the world you envision, projecting your imagination into matter – however you want to put it – at bottom all of those phrases are summed up by this provocative phrase: 'becoming God on earth.'

I understand that many people have a serious problem with a phrase like that. Mainstream religions, for one, have a problem with it, considering it outright blasphemy to call oneself God or even to claim that you are a 'part' of God, in some sense. Mainstream science also has a serious problem with that phrase, claiming there is no evidence that our wills, intentions, or minds can influence the world of matter much less create it in all its glory. Indeed, for most people in most walks of life, this would be the talk of hocus-pocus and hucksterism, of insane delusion.

You, the reader, must right away come to terms with you how feel about the above state of affairs. That's your first priority.

In concluding my essay, I now come full circle to note a very curious fact about Western civilization: since the Renaissance (if not long before), the totality of our civilization's knowledge has been ***split***, as it were, between two lineages of thinkers who refuse to cooperate and work together and who barely acknowledge the existence of each other most of the time.

On the one hand, we have the lineage described in Part I of this essay, the lineage we might call 'Western academic philosophy.' On the other hand, we have the lineage whose basic philosophy of a creative will or intention I've touched upon in Part II of this essay, the lineage we might call 'Western esotericism' or 'Western occultism.'

While those two lineages have coexisted for many centuries, only the former has achieved cultural canonization, in the sense that its representatives (Descartes, Locke, Hume, Kant, Hegel, Marx, Nietzsche, Wittgenstein, among many others) are read and studied in universities throughout the Western world. As for the latter 'occult' lineage, its representatives (Henry Cornelius Agrippa, Madame Blavatsky, Eliphas Levi, Paschal Beverly Randolph, Aleister Crowley, Dion Fortune, G.I. Gurdjieff, L. Ron Hubbard, among others), in both life and death, have drawn only derision from the academy.

The specific reasons for this derision are many and varied. But the bottom line is that the two lineages operate within systems of belief that are logically incompatible. In particular, Western academic philosophy and, by extension, Western empirical science have refused and continue to refuse to accept the belief that 'will (or mind) directly influences matter,' a belief that, in some form or other, is central to all schools of ancient and modern esoteric thought.

Academic philosophy and science will tell you they refuse to accept that belief because there is not a shred of evidence in support of it. But what they don't tell you is that there never can be a shred of evidence in support of that belief because the words 'will' and 'mind' are by definition non-evident and therefore by definition not detectable by the senses or scientific instrumentation. The only logical conclusion to draw from this state of affairs is that, from the perspective of academic philosophy and empirical science, it is indeterminate whether will (or mind) does or does not directly influence matter. Nonetheless, science typically insists that belief is false.

While that may sound like a rather technical point, in fact it beautifully illustrates the confused and disturbed attitude academic philosophy and science have toward non-evident entities like 'mind,' 'will,' 'God,' 'spirit,' and 'soul.' In contrast, Western occult traditions have concentrated much of their attention on exactly those non-evident entities, even developing techniques and methods they claim allow direct, non-sensory knowledge of them.

Thus the 'knowledge split' I discuss here finally comes down to radically different *beliefs* between occultists and scientists concerning non-evident entities.

In any case, it is my hope that this essay shows how those two lineages are, in fact, not only compatible but actually 'need' one another if we are to build a new knowledge base and a new civilization founded on a unity in diversity. I believe I have shown in Parts I and II how the skeptical reasoning process of Western academic philosophy logically leads us, if we are willing to follow it, to the creativity of the willed imagination celebrated by Western occultism.

The doctrine and method that allow those two apparently unrelated and conflicting lineages of endeavor to unite into a sequential stream of activity is the method skeptical nihilism, described in this essay as well as in my other two essays, *Aiming Higher Than Mere Civilization* and *Beyond Words & Machines.*

www.ingramcontent.com/pod-product-compliance
Lightning Source LLC
Chambersburg PA
CBHW061743020426
42331CB00006B/1336
9780692502167